Plantain Cookbook

Mouthwatering plantain recipes around the world

Laurent Cuisiner

Contents:

Sri Lankan Plantain Curry (Ala Kesel Muwa)

Plantain Rissoles - A Tropical Twist on a Classic

Brazilian Plantain Chip Rolls (Roladinhos de Banana-da-Terra)

Jamaican Spicy Plantain Croquettes

Filipino Plantain Croquettes (Maruya)

Argentinian Plantain Croquettes (Croquetas de Plátano)

Vietnamese Sweet Plantain Dessert (Chuối Sứ Ở)

Kenyan Plantain Banana Bread

Haitian Plantain Beignets (Banann Peze)

Jamaican Fried Green Plantains (Tostones)

Indonesian Fried Plantain Waffles (Wafel Pisang Goreng)

Costa Rican-Style Fried Plantains (Patacones)

Ugandan Plantain Cassava Fufu

South Indian Plantain Cassava Dosa

Nigerian Plantain Eba (Amala Ogede)

Portuguese Plantain Fries (Batatas Fritas de Platano)

Canadian Plantain Poutine

Japanese Plantain Tempura

Puerto Rican Fried Green Plantain Pies (Pastelillos de Plátano Verde)

Guatemalan Stuffed Plantain Leaves (Tamales de Plátano)

Colombian Plantain Tostones (Patacones)

Italian Plantain Pizza (Pizza di Platano)

Ghanaian Plantain Porridge (Mutufu Ekado)

French Plantain Gratin (Gratin de Plantain)

Italian Plantain Gnocchi (Gnocchi di Platano)

Mexican Plantain Sopes

Turkish Plantain Kofte

Indian Plantain Kachori

American Plantain Grilled Cheese

Introduction

The humble plantain, a staple in many cultures around the world, takes center stage in the exciting realm of the plantain cookbook. This culinary guide unlocks a treasure trove of delicious possibilities, transforming this versatile ingredient into a myriad of delectable dishes.

Imagine embarking on a global adventure with each turn of the page. One recipe might whisk you away to the vibrant markets of Latin America, where savory fried plantains known as "tostones" are a beloved street food.

The next recipe could transport you to the sun-drenched shores of the Caribbean, where sweet and fragrant plantain fritters, fragrant with rum and spices, tantalize your taste buds.

Perhaps you'll find yourself exploring the rich tapestry of African cuisine, where plantains are mashed into creamy fufu, a staple accompaniment to stews and soups.

The beauty of a plantain cookbook lies in its ability to bridge cultures and continents. Within its pages, you'll discover:

A Comprehensive Guide to Plantains: Explore the different varieties of plantains, their unique characteristics, and how to select the perfect level of ripeness for each recipe.

Fundamental Cooking Techniques: Master essential techniques like frying, boiling, and mashing, all tailored to unlock the full potential of plantains.

A Spectrum of Flavorful Dishes: From savory appetizers and side dishes to soul-satisfying main courses and irresistible desserts, the plantain cookbook offers a world of culinary inspiration.

Vegetarian and Vegan Options: Many plantain recipes are naturally vegetarian or vegan, making this a perfect cookbook for those seeking plant-based culinary adventures.

Whether you're a seasoned cook or a curious explorer of new flavors, the plantain cookbook is your passport to a delicious adventure. So, grab your apron, unleash your creativity, and embark on a culinary journey with this versatile and exciting ingredient!

The Global Journey of the Plantain: From Ancient Staple to Modern Favorite

The plantain's journey to becoming a global food is a fascinating tale of exploration, trade, and cultural exchange. Here's a glimpse into its history:

Ancient Origins (500 BC): Evidence suggests plantains were first domesticated in Southeast Asia, likely around Malaysia and Indonesia. Eastward Expansion: Through trade routes, plantains traveled to India, possibly introduced by traders. Alexander the Great's conquests might have further spread them westward.

African Encounter (Unknown Date): The exact timeline is unclear, but plantains eventually reached Africa, likely through Arab and Asian merchants. They quickly became a vital source of carbohydrates and nutrients for many African cultures.

The Columbian Exchange (15th Century): Portuguese explorers are credited with introducing plantains to the Caribbean and Latin America during the Columbian Exchange. This period saw a massive exchange of plants and animals between the Americas, Europe, and Africa.

A Global Staple: Plantains thrived in the tropical climates of these new regions, becoming a staple food source. Their versatility and long shelf life when cooked (unlike dessert bananas) made them ideal for long voyages and exploration.

Factors Contributing to Global Spread:

Trade and Exploration: Plantains were a valuable commodity, easily transported and adaptable to different environments. Trade routes played a crucial role in spreading them across continents.

Cultural Exchange: As people migrated and interacted, they brought their food traditions with them. This led to the adoption of plantains in various cuisines around the world.

Adaptability: Plantains can be cooked in many ways, making them a perfect fit for diverse culinary preferences. They can be savory or sweet, fried, boiled, or mashed, offering endless possibilities.

Today, plantains are a beloved ingredient in countless cultures, from Africa and the Caribbean to Latin America and beyond. Their rich history and global reach are a testament to the power of food to connect people and places.

General health benefits of plantain

Plantains offer a surprising range of health benefits thanks to their nutrient profile. Here are some of the key advantages:

Digestive Health: Plantains are a good source of fiber, which promotes regularity and keeps your digestive system running smoothly. The resistant starch in green plantains acts as a prebiotic, feeding the good bacteria in your gut.

Heart Health: Plantains are rich in potassium, a mineral that helps regulate blood pressure and counteracts the effects of sodium. Additionally, their fiber content can help lower LDL (bad) cholesterol.

Blood Sugar Management: Unlike their sweeter cousin, the banana, plantains have a lower glycemic index (GI). This means they cause a slower rise in blood sugar, making them a good choice for people with diabetes or managing blood sugar levels.

Immune System Support: Plantains are a good source of vitamins C and A, both essential for a healthy immune system. Vitamin C helps fight off infections, while vitamin A plays a role in maintaining healthy mucous membranes, which are your body's first line of defense against germs.

Source of Essential Nutrients: Plantains are a good source of complex carbohydrates, which provide sustained energy. They also contain B vitamins, which are important for metabolism and energy production.

It's important to remember that cooking methods can impact the nutritional value of plantains. Frying them adds fat and calories, while boiling or baking them is a healthier option.

Overall, plantains are a delicious and nutritious addition to a balanced diet. They provide a range of health benefits and can be savored in numerous ways.

Nigerian Fried Plantain Delight

Introduction
Nigerian fried plantain is a delectable and versatile dish enjoyed in many West African countries. The dish features ripe or unripe plantains fried to perfection in golden-hued, fragrant oil. This recipe will guide you through the process of preparing this mouth-watering delicacy in the comfort of your kitchen.

Brief History
Plantains, known as "dodo" in Nigeria, were introduced to West Africa in the 16th century by Portuguese explorers. Over time, the plantain became a significant part of the region's cuisine, with each country adding its unique twist. Fried plantain, or dodo, remains one of Nigeria's most beloved dishes, enjoyed by millions daily.

Ingredients
2 ripe or unripe plantains
Vegetable oil for frying
Salt to taste
Optional: Cayenne pepper or chili powder

Preparation Steps
Cut the ends off the plantains and make a shallow cut along the length of each plantain, taking care not to slice through.
Peel off the skin, ensuring that you remove all traces of it.
Diagonally slice the plantains into pieces of about 1/2 to 1 inch thick.
Place a deep pan on medium heat and add oil to around 1/4 inch deep.
Once the oil is hot, carefully add the plantain slices to the pan, ensuring not to overcrowd it.
Fry the plantains for 2-3 minutes on each side until golden brown and crispy.

Remove the fried plantains from the pan using a slotted spoon and transfer them to a paper towel-lined plate to absorb the excess oil.

Sprinkle salt and optional spices (cayenne pepper or chili powder) to taste while the plantains are still warm.

Health Benefits

Fried plantains are a good source of dietary fiber, potassium, and vitamins A and C. They provide essential nutrients while satisfying your taste buds.

Storage and Reheating Information

Fried plantains can be stored in an airtight container in the refrigerator for up to 3 days. Reheat them in an oven or toaster oven at 350°F (175°C) for 5-7 minutes or until heated through and crispy again.

Anecdotes, Stories, and Quotes

A popular Nigerian proverb goes, "When the music changes, so does the dance." Similarly, the plantain's adaptability has allowed it to become an essential part of Nigerian cuisine.

Chef Evaluation

Fried plantains are a true testament to Nigeria's rich culinary heritage, offering a delightful blend of sweetness and savoriness that leaves you craving more.

Serving Suggestions

Serve Nigerian fried plantains as a side dish to accompany hearty stews, rice dishes, or bean-based dishes like moi-moi or akara. You can also enjoy them as a snack with a sprinkle of chili powder or paired with a spicy dipping sauce.

Best Time to Eat

Nigerian fried plantains are a versatile treat that can be savored at any time of the day. Enjoy them as a breakfast accompaniment, a satisfying lunch side dish, or a comforting evening snack.

Conclusion

Embark on a culinary adventure to West Africa with this Nigerian fried plantain recipe. The irresistible crunch and delightful flavors will transport you to the bustling streets of Nigeria, where food brings people together and celebrates the rich tapestry of cultures and traditions.

Tantalizing Cuban Green Plantain Fritters (Tostones de Plátano)

Introduction

Explore the flavors of Cuba with these delectable green plantain fritters, also known as Tostones de Plátano. Combining the starchy goodness of unripe plantains with the right seasonings, this dish promises an authentic taste of the Caribbean.

Brief History

Tostones de Plátano originated in Cuba, with influences from West African and Spanish cuisine. These plantain fritters have evolved over time, becoming a beloved staple in Cuban households and restaurants worldwide.

Ingredients

2 green plantains
Kosher salt, to taste
1/4 cup olive oil
Optional: Garlic sauce (mojo) or cilantro-garlic sauce (mojo de cilantro)

Preparation Steps

Cut the ends off the plantains and slice a shallow line down the side, taking care not to cut through.

Remove the peel from the plantains.

Slice the plantains into 1-inch thick rounds.

Warm olive oil in a sizable skillet on medium-high heat.

Fry the plantain slices until golden brown on both sides (about 2-3 minutes per side).

Remove the fried plantain slices from the skillet and place them on a paper towel-lined plate.

Allow the slices to cool slightly, then flatten them using a plantain press or a wooden cutting board (cover the slices with parchment paper before flattening).

Reintroduce the flattened plantain pieces into the heated oil and cook for an additional 2-3 minutes, or until they achieve a crispy, golden texture.Transfer the fried fritters to a paper towel-lined plate and sprinkle with salt while still warm.

Serve hot, either plain or with garlic sauce (mojo) or cilantro-garlic sauce (mojo de cilantro).

Health Benefits
Green plantains are rich in fiber, potassium, and vitamins A and C, offering potential health benefits such as improved digestion, heart health, and immune system support.

Storage and Reheating Information
Place any remaining fritters in a sealed container and store them in the fridge for a maximum of three days. Reheat them in an oven or toaster oven at 350°F (175°C) for 5-7 minutes or until heated through and crispy again.

Anecdotes, Stories, and Quotes
As Cuban writer José Martí once said, "The happiness of a people is like a plant that grows and flourishes in the soil of liberty." Similarly,

the rich and diverse flavors of Cuban cuisine, like Tostones de Plátano, bring people together and nourish the soul.

Chef Evaluation

These green plantain fritters offer a delightful balance of flavors and textures, making them the perfect introduction to the wonders of Cuban cuisine. Their crunchy exterior gives way to a soft, savory center that pairs perfectly with traditional sauces and dips.

Serving Suggestions

Serve Tostones de Plátano as an appetizer or side dish alongside traditional Cuban dishes like ropa vieja or arroz con pollo. Alternatively, enjoy them as a snack with garlic sauce (mojo) or cilantro-garlic sauce (mojo de cilantro).

Best Time to Eat

These crispy fritters are a versatile treat that can be savored at any time of the day, whether as a brunch addition, a satisfying lunch side dish, or a delightful evening snack.

Conclusion

Transport your taste buds to the sunny shores of Cuba with this authentic recipe for green plantain fritters (Tostones de Plátano). Experience the joy of bringing a small piece of Cuban culture to life in your kitchen, and relish the unforgettable flavors that define this Caribbean gem.

Puerto Rican Plantain Empanadas
(Empanadas de Platano)

Introduction
Experience the vibrant flavors of Puerto Rico with these savory plantain empanadas, known as Empanadas de Platano. This delightful dish brings together the natural sweetness of ripe plantains and a flavorful beef filling that will transport your taste buds to the sunny shores of the Caribbean.

Brief History
Empanadas de Platano have been a beloved staple in Puerto Rican cuisine for generations. These delicious empanadas combine Spanish and African culinary influences, showcasing the rich cultural heritage of the island.

Ingredients

4 ripe plantains

1 lb ground beef

1 small onion, diced

1/2 bell pepper, diced

2 cloves garlic, minced

1 tsp cumin

Salt and pepper, to taste

Oil for frying

Preparation Steps
Peel the plantains and cut them into large chunks.

Blend the plantain chunks in a food processor or mash them by hand until a smooth, dough-like consistency is achieved.

In a skillet, cook the ground beef with onions, bell peppers, garlic, cumin, salt, and pepper until the meat is browned and the vegetables are tender.

Remove the meat mixture from heat and let it cool.

Form small balls (about 2 inches in diameter) with the plantain dough.

Using a tortilla press or your hands, flatten each ball into a small disc (about 1/8-inch thick).

Place a spoonful of the cooled meat mixture in the center of each plantain disc.

Fold the dough in half, creating a half-moon shape, and seal the edges with a fork or by folding them over onto themselves.

In a deep skillet or saucepan, heat the oil to 350°F (175°C).

Carefully place the empanadas into the hot oil and fry until golden brown on both sides (about 2-3 minutes per side).

Take out the empanadas from the oil and transfer them to a plate lined with paper towels to absorb any extra oil.

Serve hot, and enjoy!

Health Benefits

Plantains offer various health benefits, including high amounts of fiber and potassium. In addition, the inclusion of vegetables in the meat filling adds extra nutrients to this dish.

Storage and Reheating Information

Store leftover empanadas in an airtight container in the refrigerator for up to 3 days. Reheat them in an oven or toaster oven at 350°F (175°C) for 5-7 minutes or until heated through and crispy again.

Anecdotes, Stories, and Quotes

The famous Puerto Rican poet Lola Rodríguez de Tió once said, "Puerto Rico is a beautiful and beloved island with its unique culture, beautiful landscape, and friendly people." These plantain empanadas encapsulate the warmth and vibrancy of Puerto Rican culture and cuisine.

Chef Evaluation

Empanadas de Platano are a delightful fusion of flavors that will satisfy any palate. The sweetness of the ripe plantain dough contrasts beautifully with the savory beef filling, creating an unforgettable gastronomic experience.

Serving Suggestions

Serve these empanadas as a main dish, appetizer, or snack, accompanied by a refreshing tropical fruit salsa or a spicy mayo-ketchup sauce for dipping.

Best Time to Eat

Empanadas de Platano can be enjoyed at any time of day, whether for breakfast, lunch, dinner, or even as a late-night snack.

Conclusion

Indulge in the rich flavors of Puerto Rico with these authentic plantain empanadas. This recipe showcases the best of the island's culinary heritage and offers a taste of Puerto Rican culture that will leave you craving more.

Ghanaian Plantain Porridge (Abakate Kwan)

Introduction
Immerse yourself in the flavors of Ghana with this comforting plantain porridge recipe, known locally as Abakate Kwan. This hearty dish combines ripe plantains, aromatic spices, and a variety of flavorful ingredients to create a deliciously satisfying bowl that is perfect for any time of day.

Brief History
Abakate Kwan is a traditional Ghanaian dish that highlights the culinary creativity and resourcefulness of the local people. Plantains have been a staple in Ghanaian cuisine for generations and are used in various dishes, showcasing the country's diverse culinary heritage.

Ingredients
2 ripe plantains
1/2 onion, diced
1/2 bell pepper, diced
2 cloves garlic, minced
1 medium tomato, chopped
1/2 tsp ginger, grated
1/2 tsp chili powder or cayenne pepper
1/2 tsp salt
2 cups water
2 tbsp palm oil
Optional: smoked fish, crab, or shrimp

Preparation Steps
Peel the plantains and chop them into small pieces.

In a blender or food processor, blend the plantains into a smooth paste.

In a sizable pot, warm the palm oil over medium heat.

Add onions, bell peppers, garlic, and ginger, and cook for 3-4 minutes until the vegetables soften.

Stir in the chopped tomatoes and cook for an additional 2-3 minutes.

Add the chili powder or cayenne pepper and salt to the pot and mix well.

Gradually add water to the pot while stirring to create a smooth consistency.

Stir in the blended plantain paste, mixing well to prevent lumps from forming.

Reduce heat and let the porridge simmer for 10-15 minutes, stirring occasionally, until it reaches your desired thickness.

If you're adding seafood, place the smoked fish, crab, or shrimp in the pot and cook for an additional 5 minutes.

Serve the plantain porridge hot, garnished with your choice of fresh herbs, nuts, or additional spices.

Health Benefits
Plantains are rich in fiber, potassium, and vitamins A and C, making them a nutritious addition to any meal. The inclusion of vegetables and optional seafood also adds essential nutrients to this dish.

Storage and Reheating Information

Store leftover plantain porridge in an airtight container in the refrigerator for up to 3 days. Reheat in a saucepan over low heat, stirring occasionally and adding a little water if needed to reach the desired consistency.

Anecdotes, Stories, and Quotes

Ghanaian writer and poet Kofi Awoonor once said, "The plantain tree is our poetry; its fruit is the history of our people." Abakate Kwan beautifully exemplifies this sentiment, showcasing the importance of plantains in Ghanaian cuisine and culture.

Chef Evaluation

Abakate Kwan is a warm and comforting dish that offers a delightful blend of sweet and savory flavors. Its versatility allows you to adapt the recipe to suit your taste and dietary preferences, making it a perfect addition to any menu.

Serving Suggestions

Serve Ghanaian plantain porridge as a main dish or side dish, pairing it with grilled meats, stews, or salads for a balanced meal.

Best Time to Eat

Enjoy Abakate Kwan for breakfast, lunch, or dinner, as its comforting flavor and adaptable nature make it suitable for any time of day.

Conclusion

Discover the heartwarming flavors of Ghana with this authentic plantain porridge recipe. Abakate Kwan offers a unique taste of the country's rich culinary tradition and a delightful way to explore the diverse cuisines of West Africa.

Trinidadian Plantain Roti

Introduction
Embark on a culinary adventure to Trinidad and Tobago with this unique plantain roti recipe. Combining the versatility of ripe plantains and the traditional art of roti-making, this dish offers a delightful fusion of flavors that is sure to impress.

Brief History
Plantain roti is a creative twist on the classic Trinidadian roti, which has roots in Indian cuisine. As generations of Indian immigrants settled in Trinidad and Tobago, they adapted traditional dishes using local ingredients, such as plantains, giving birth to this innovative and delicious flatbread.

Ingredients
2 ripe plantains
2 cups all-purpose flour
1/2 tsp baking powder
1/2 tsp salt
1/4 cup vegetable oil
Water, as needed

Preparation Steps
Mash the ripe plantains until smooth.

In a large mixing bowl, combine the mashed plantains, flour, baking powder, and salt.

Gradually add oil to the mixture while mixing with your hands or a wooden spoon to form a crumbly texture.

Slowly add water, a little at a time, and continue mixing until a soft dough forms. Massage the dough for approximately 5 minutes until it reaches a smooth and elastic texture.

Divide the dough into small balls (about the size of a lime).

On a surface lightly dusted with flour, flatten each ball of dough into a thin circle, measuring around 8 inches in diameter.

Place the rolled-out plantain roti on the heated skillet and let it cook until small bubbles form on the surface and the bottom begins to brown, about 1-2 minutes.

Flip the roti and cook the other side until it's golden brown and cooked through.

Remove the cooked roti from the skillet and place it on a plate, covering it with a clean kitchen towel to keep it warm and soft.

Repeat the process of rolling and cooking with the remaining dough balls.

Serve warm plantain roti with your choice of curries, stews, or vegetable dishes.

Health Benefits

Plantains are high in fiber and potassium, contributing to better digestive health and promoting heart health. Additionally, this plantain roti recipe is vegan-friendly, making it a suitable choice for those following a plant-based diet.

Storage and Reheating Information

Store leftover plantain roti in an airtight container or wrapped in plastic wrap for up to 2 days. Reheat in a skillet or microwave until warm and pliable before serving.

Anecdotes, Stories, and Quotes

Trinidadian writer and historian C.L.R. James once said, "Cooking is like life. It's all about experimenting and making something beautiful out of simple ingredients." Plantain roti exemplifies this philosophy, showcasing how culinary creativity can result in a unique and delicious dish.

Chef Evaluation

Plantain roti is a unique and versatile flatbread that offers a taste of Trinidad and Tobago's rich culinary heritage. Its soft texture and subtle sweetness make it an excellent accompaniment to a wide array of dishes.

Serving Suggestions

Serve Trinidadian plantain roti with traditional curries, such as chicken or chickpea curry, or use it as a wrap for salads and grilled vegetables.

Best Time to Eat

Plantain roti can be enjoyed at any time of day, whether as a breakfast wrap, a lunchtime companion to flavorful stews, or a delicious addition to your dinner spread.

Conclusion

Bring a taste of Trinidad and Tobago's diverse culinary heritage to your table with this plantain roti recipe. Experience the joy of creating something extraordinary from humble ingredients and savor the mouthwatering flavors of the Caribbean.

South African Plantain Pancakes

Introduction

Discover the delightful world of South African cuisine with these plantain pancakes, a unique twist on a classic breakfast favorite. Combining the natural sweetness of ripe plantains and traditional pancake ingredients, this recipe offers a delicious and wholesome start to your day.

Brief History

South African plantain pancakes highlight the culinary fusion that has evolved through centuries of diverse cultural influences. The introduction of plantains to South Africa can be traced back to colonial times, and their incorporation into local dishes showcases the adaptability and innovation of South African cooks.

Ingredients

2 ripe plantains
1 cup all-purpose flour
1/2 tsp baking powder
1/4 tsp salt
1/2 cup milk
1 large egg
2 tbsp sugar
1 tsp vanilla extract
Oil or butter for cooking

Preparation Steps

Mash the ripe plantains until smooth.

In a mixing bowl, whisk together flour, baking powder, and salt.

In a separate bowl, mix milk, egg, sugar, vanilla extract, and mashed plantains until well combined.

Gradually add the wet ingredients to the dry ingredients, whisking until a smooth batter is formed.

Warm a skillet or griddle over medium heat and lightly coat it with oil or butter.

Pour approximately 1/4 cup of batter onto the heated skillet for each pancake.

Cook the pancakes for about 2-3 minutes until small bubbles appear on the surface and the edges begin to set.

Flip the pancakes and cook for an additional 1-2 minutes until golden brown and cooked through.

Remove the cooked pancakes from the skillet and keep them warm while cooking the remaining batter.

Serve the plantain pancakes warm with your choice of toppings, such as fresh fruit, honey, or syrup.

Health Benefits

Plantains are a good source of fiber and potassium, which contribute to digestive health and heart health. This plantain pancake recipe offers a more nutritious alternative to traditional pancakes by incorporating fruits into your breakfast.

Storage and Reheating Information

Store leftover plantain pancakes in an airtight container in the refrigerator for up to 3 days. Reheat them in a toaster or microwave until warm before serving.

Anecdotes, Stories, and Quotes

Nelson Mandela once said, "The food we eat tells a story of who we are and where we come from." South African plantain pancakes encapsulate this sentiment, showcasing the country's rich culinary heritage and innovative spirit.

Chef Evaluation

South African plantain pancakes offer a delightful fusion of flavors that will elevate your breakfast experience. Their natural sweetness and light, fluffy texture make them an excellent canvas for various toppings and a satisfying dish for any palate.

Serving Suggestions

Enjoy these plantain pancakes for breakfast or brunch, topped with fresh seasonal fruits, a drizzle of honey, or a dollop of whipped cream.

Best Time to Eat

Savor South African plantain pancakes during breakfast or brunch, when their warm and comforting flavor will provide a satisfying start to your day.

Conclusion

South African plantain pancakes offer a unique and delectable twist on a classic dish. Experience the rich and vibrant flavors of South Africa with this recipe and create new culinary memories to cherish.

Dominican Plantain Tostones

Introduction
Embark on a culinary adventure to the Dominican Republic with this classic plantain tostones recipe. These crispy, golden plantain delights offer a delightful texture and flavor that make them a versatile and beloved side dish in Caribbean cuisine.

Brief History
Tostones have their roots in African cuisine and were later adapted in the Caribbean, including the Dominican Republic. Their enduring popularity is a testament to their rich history and the diverse cultural influences that have shaped the culinary landscape of the region.

Ingredients
2 unripe (green) plantains
Oil for frying
Salt to taste
Optional: garlic, chili powder, or lime wedges

Preparation Steps
Slice the ends off the plantains and make a shallow cut down the side to peel off the skin.

Cut the peeled plantains into thick slices, approximately 1 inch each. Heat about 2 inches of oil in a heavy-bottomed pan or skillet over medium heat.

Carefully place the plantain slices into the heated oil, ensuring not to overcrowd the pan.

Fry the plantain slices for about 2-3 minutes on each side until they turn a light golden color.

Remove the plantain slices from the oil and place them on a paper towel-lined plate to drain any excess oil.

Using a flat object, like a tostonera or a wooden cutting board, flatten each plantain slice to about half its thickness.

Return the flattened plantain slices to the heated oil and fry them again for 2-3 minutes until they become crisp and golden brown.

Transfer the fried tostones to a paper towel-lined plate to absorb any excess oil.

Sprinkle salt over the tostones while they're still warm.

Optionally, serve with garlic, chili powder, or lime wedges for added flavor.

Health Benefits
Plantains are rich in fiber, potassium, and vitamins A and C, contributing to overall health and well-being. Frying them twice reduces their moisture content and enhances their crispiness, offering a satisfying and flavorful snack or side dish.

Storage and Reheating Information
Plantain tostones are best served immediately after frying to enjoy their crisp texture. Keep any remaining portions in an airtight container in the refrigerator for a maximum of 2 days. Reheat in a toaster oven or oven until heated through and crisp.

Anecdotes, Stories, and Quotes

In her book "The Latin American Cookbook," author Daisy Martinez shares, "Plantains are to Latin American cuisine what potatoes are to North Americans." Plantain tostones perfectly encapsulate this sentiment, offering a delicious and versatile dish rooted in the diverse culinary traditions of the Dominican Republic.

Chef Evaluation

Dominican plantain tostones provide a delightful blend of flavor and texture that complements various dishes. Their crispy exterior and soft interior make them a versatile and satisfying addition to any meal.

Serving Suggestions

Enjoy plantain tostones as a side dish or appetizer, pairing them with garlic dipping sauce, chimichurri, or fresh salsa for added flavor.

Best Time to Eat

Plantain tostones can be enjoyed at any time of day, either as a snack or alongside your favorite main dishes for a satisfying meal.

Conclusion

Dominican plantain tostones offer a delightful and flavorful journey into Caribbean cuisine. Embrace the unique flavors and textures of this classic dish and experience the rich culinary traditions that have captivated palates for generations.

Peruvian Plantain Polenta

Introduction
Take your palate on a Peruvian adventure with this plantain polenta recipe. A fusion of traditional polenta and the flavors of ripe plantains, this dish offers a unique and versatile side that perfectly complements various stews, sauces, and grilled meats.

Brief History
Polenta has its roots in Italian cuisine and has been embraced by various cultures worldwide. In Peru, plantains are widely used in local dishes due to their availability and versatility, inspiring this innovative plantain polenta recipe that showcases the fusion of cultures and ingredients in Peruvian cuisine.

Ingredients
2 ripe plantains
2 cups water
1/2 cup cornmeal
2 tbsp unsalted butter
Salt to taste
Optional: grated cheese (such as Parmesan or Queso Fresco) for serving

Preparation Steps
Mash the ripe plantains until smooth.

In a medium saucepan, bring the water to a boil.

Gradually whisk in the cornmeal, ensuring no lumps form.

Reduce heat to low and continue whisking the mixture until it begins to thicken, about 2-3 minutes.

Add the mashed plantains to the cornmeal mixture, stirring until well combined.

Continue cooking over low heat, stirring occasionally, until the polenta reaches a creamy consistency, about 15-20 minutes.

Stir in butter and season with salt to taste.

If desired, stir in grated cheese until it melts and incorporates into the polenta.

Serve the plantain polenta warm, topped with additional cheese or your choice of sauces and stews.

Health Benefits
Plantains are rich in fiber and potassium, offering various health benefits. Incorporating them into polenta enhances the nutritional value of this dish, making it a healthier alternative to traditional polenta.

Storage and Reheating Information
Store leftover plantain polenta in an airtight container in the refrigerator for up to 3 days. To reheat, add a small amount of water or milk and warm the polenta in a saucepan over low heat, stirring frequently until heated through.

Anecdotes, Stories, and Quotes
Peruvian chef Gastón Acurio has famously said, "Peruvian cuisine is a beautiful fusion of cultures." Plantain polenta perfectly embodies this

notion, showcasing the culinary creativity that results from merging diverse traditions and flavors.

Chef Evaluation
Plantain polenta offers a versatile and flavorful base for various Peruvian-inspired dishes. Its creamy texture and subtle sweetness make it an ideal pairing for a variety of savory stews and sauces.

Serving Suggestions
Serve plantain polenta as a side dish, complementing it with flavorful stews, such as Peruvian-style beef or chicken stews, or grilled meats and vegetables.

Best Time to Eat
Plantain polenta can be enjoyed any time of day, from a hearty breakfast to a satisfying dinner side. Pair it with your favorite Peruvian-inspired dishes for a complete and delightful meal.

Conclusion
Experience the unique fusion of Peruvian flavors and traditions with this plantain polenta recipe. Delight in the creamy texture and subtle sweetness of this versatile dish that pays homage to the culinary heritage of Peru.

Mexican Plantain Tamales

Introduction

Embark on a flavorful journey to Mexico with these plantain tamales, a unique twist on the traditional tamal. Combining the sweetness of ripe plantains with the savory flavors of corn masa, these tamales offer a delightful and authentic taste of Mexican cuisine.

Brief History

Tamales have been a staple of Mesoamerican cuisine since ancient times, with various fillings and wrappings used throughout history. Incorporating plantains into tamales showcases the adaptability and creativity of Mexican cooks in using ingredients available in the region.

Ingredients

2 ripe plantains
2 cups masa harina (corn flour)
1/2 cup lard or vegetable shortening
1 tsp baking powder
1 tsp salt
2 cups chicken broth or vegetable broth
Dried corn husks

Preparation Steps

Soak corn husks in hot water for at least 30 minutes until softened.

Mash the ripe plantains until smooth.

In a large mixing bowl, combine masa harina, lard, baking powder, and salt.

Mix the ingredients with your hands or a stand mixer until the texture resembles coarse crumbs.

Gradually add the chicken broth while mixing until a smooth dough forms.

Stir in the mashed plantains, ensuring they are well incorporated into the dough.

Drain the soaked corn husks and pat them dry with paper towels.

To assemble the tamales, spread a thin layer of the plantain dough onto the center of a corn husk.

Fold the sides of the corn husk over the dough, then fold the bottom up to encase the filling.

Tie the tamales with kitchen twine or strips of corn husk to secure them.

Arrange the tamales in a steamer basket, standing them upright with the folded side facing up.

Steam the tamales for about 1 hour, checking periodically and adding more water to the steamer if needed.

Remove the cooked tamales from the steamer and let them cool slightly before serving.

Health Benefits
Plantains offer a wealth of nutrients, including fiber and potassium, which contribute to digestive health and heart health. Combining

them with the corn masa provides a satisfying and balanced dish that's both flavorful and nutritious.

Storage and Reheating Information
Store leftover plantain tamales in an airtight container in the refrigerator for up to 3 days. Reheat them by steaming for about 15-20 minutes or microwaving until heated through.

Anecdotes, Stories, and Quotes
Mexican chef and author Diana Sánchez has said, "Mexican cuisine is like a beautiful mosaic of colors, flavors, and ingredients." Plantain tamales are a perfect example of this, showcasing the richness and diversity of the country's culinary traditions.

Chef Evaluation
Plantain tamales offer a unique and delightful twist on the classic tamal. Their sweet and savory flavors, combined with the soft, tender texture, make them an ideal addition to any Mexican-inspired meal.

Serving Suggestions
Enjoy plantain tamales as a main dish or side, accompanied by your choice of salsas, crema, cheese, or beans. Pair with a refreshing agua fresca for a complete culinary experience.

Best Time to Eat
Traditionally served during holidays and special occasions, plantain tamales can be enjoyed any time of day, from breakfast to dinner. Share them with friends and family for a memorable and delicious meal.

Conclusion

Experience the delightful fusion of flavors in Mexican plantain tamales, a creative and tasty twist on a traditional dish. Embrace the culinary heritage of Mexico and delight in these sweet, savory, and satisfying treats.

Indian Plantain Fritters (Kache Kele Ki Tikki)

Introduction

Embark on an enticing Indian culinary adventure with these plantain fritters, a delectable and popular street food known as Kache Kele Ki Tikki. This flavorful dish combines the sweetness of ripe plantains with aromatic Indian spices, resulting in a mouthwatering treat that's perfect for snacking or serving as a side dish.

Brief History

Indian cuisine boasts a rich and diverse history, with plantains playing a significant role in various regional dishes. Kache Kele Ki Tikki demonstrates the inventive use of plantains in Indian cooking, showcasing the country's vibrant culinary traditions.

Ingredients

2 ripe plantains
1/2 cup chickpea flour (besan)
1/2 tsp red chili powder
1/2 tsp cumin powder
1/2 tsp coriander powder
1/2 tsp salt
Oil for frying

Preparation Steps

Mash the ripe plantains until smooth.

Mix chickpea flour, red chili powder, cumin powder, coriander powder, and salt with the mashed plantains until well combined.

Form the mixture into small, flattened fritters.

Heat oil in a heavy-bottomed pan or skillet over medium heat. Carefully place the plantain fritters into the heated oil, ensuring not to overcrowd the pan.

Fry the fritters for approximately 2-3 minutes on each side until they achieve a golden brown and crispy texture.

Take out the cooked fritters from the oil and transfer them to a plate lined with paper towels to absorb any extra oil.

Serve the plantain fritters warm, with your choice of chutneys or sauces.

Health Benefits
Plantains are rich in fiber and potassium, offering various health benefits. Incorporating them into these flavorful fritters provides a delicious and satisfying snack or side dish that's both nutritious and enjoyable.

Storage and Reheating Information
Store leftover plantain fritters in an airtight container in the refrigerator for up to 2 days. Reheat them in a preheated oven or toaster oven until heated through and crispy before serving.

Anecdotes, Stories, and Quotes
Indian chef and cookbook author Madhur Jaffrey once said, "Indian food is like a vast ocean; the deeper you go, the more treasures you find." Plantain fritters exemplify this sentiment, showcasing the inventive use of ingredients and flavors in Indian cuisine.

Chef Evaluation

Kache Kele Ki Tikki offers a delightful balance of sweet and savory flavors with a satisfyingly crispy texture. These plantain fritters are a versatile and tasty addition to any Indian-inspired meal or snack.

Serving Suggestions

Enjoy plantain fritters as a snack or appetizer, pairing them with your favorite chutneys, such as mint or tamarind, or a refreshing raita.

Best Time to Eat

Savor Indian plantain fritters as a mid-day snack or appetizer, or pair them with your favorite curries and rice dishes for a satisfying and delicious meal.

Conclusion

Embrace the rich flavors and aromas of Indian cuisine with these delightful plantain fritters. Experience the culinary heritage of India and relish the unique combination of sweet plantains and fragrant spices in every bite.

Cameroonian Plantain Fufu

Introduction
Experience the rich culinary traditions of Cameroon with this plantain fufu recipe, a starchy and versatile side dish that pairs beautifully with soups, stews, and sauces. Plantain fufu is a delightful variation of the classic West African dish, showcasing the innovative use of ingredients in the region.

Brief History
Fufu is a staple in various West African countries, with a long-standing history in the region's culinary heritage. Plantains, a widely available and versatile ingredient, have been incorporated into fufu as a tasty alternative to cassava, yams, or maize.

Ingredients
4 unripe (green) plantains
Water for boiling

Preparation Steps
Cut the ends off the plantains and make a shallow cut down the side to peel off the skin.

Slice the peeled plantains into small, even-sized pieces.

Bring a sizable pot of water to a boil over high heat.

Add the plantain slices to the boiling water and cook until tender, about 15-20 minutes.

Drain the cooked plantains and place them in a mortar or food processor.

Mash the plantains until a smooth, sticky dough forms, gradually adding small amounts of hot water as needed to achieve the desired consistency.

Shape the plantain fufu into small balls or scoop with a spoon to serve alongside your favorite soups and stews.

Health Benefits
Unripe plantains are a rich source of fiber, potassium, and resistant starch, contributing to improved digestion and overall health. Plantain fufu offers a nutritious and satisfying side dish that complements a variety of flavorful dishes.

Storage and Reheating Information
Plantain fufu is best served fresh and warm. Keep any remaining portions in an airtight container in the refrigerator for a maximum of 2 days. To reheat, warm the fufu in a microwave-safe dish with a splash of water until heated through.

Anecdotes, Stories, and Quotes
Cameroonian chef and culinary ambassador Christian Abégan once noted, "Cameroonian cuisine is a reflection of the country's cultural diversity." Plantain fufu highlights this diversity, showcasing the adaptation of classic dishes with ingredients that are readily available.

Chef Evaluation
Plantain fufu offers a unique and flavorful variation on the classic West African dish, providing a perfect canvas for absorbing the flavors of various soups and stews. Its starchy texture and subtle plantain flavor make it an ideal side for a wide array of savory dishes.

Serving Suggestions

Enjoy plantain fufu alongside rich and flavorful Cameroonian soups, such as Ndolé or Peanut Soup, allowing the fufu to soak up the enticing flavors.

Best Time to Eat

Plantain fufu is typically enjoyed during lunch or dinner, paired with traditional soups or stews for a complete and satisfying meal.

Conclusion

Immerse yourself in the vibrant flavors of Cameroon with this plantain fufu recipe. Experience the rich culinary heritage of West Africa and delight in the versatile, starchy side that perfectly complements an array of soups and stews.

Sri Lankan Plantain Curry (Ala Kesel Muwa)

Introduction
Delight your taste buds with this flavorful and aromatic plantain curry from Sri Lanka, a dish known as Ala Kesel Muwa. Featuring the natural sweetness of ripe plantains balanced with rich spices, this curry offers a delectable and authentic taste of Sri Lankan cuisine.

Brief History
Sri Lanka is renowned for its diverse array of curries, featuring a range of ingredients and flavors that showcase the island's rich culinary heritage. Plantains have long been integrated into Sri Lankan dishes, with plantain curry offering a delicious and nutritious vegetarian option.

Ingredients
2 ripe plantains
1 small onion, finely chopped
1 tsp minced garlic
1 tsp minced ginger
1 tsp curry powder
1/2 tsp turmeric
1/2 tsp chili powder
1 cup coconut milk
Salt to taste
Coconut oil for cooking

Preparation Steps
Cut the plantains into bite-sized pieces.

Warm the coconut oil in a medium saucepan over medium heat.

Fry the chopped onions until they become translucent, about 2-3 minutes.

Add garlic and ginger, stirring for an additional minute until fragrant.

Stir in the curry powder, turmeric, and chili powder, allowing the spices to toast for 30 seconds.

Add the plantain pieces to the pan, gently stirring to coat them in the spices.

Add the coconut milk to the pot and season it with salt according to your taste.

Bring the mixture to a simmer, then reduce heat to low, allowing the curry to thicken and the plantains to become tender, about 15-20 minutes.

Serve the plantain curry warm, accompanied by rice or your choice of sides.

Health Benefits
Ripe plantains are rich in vitamins, minerals, and fiber, offering a nutritious and flavorful base for this curry. Combined with the antioxidant properties of spices like turmeric and garlic, plantain curry contributes to a balanced and healthful diet.

Storage and Reheating Information
Store any leftover plantain curry in an airtight container in the refrigerator for up to 3 days. Reheat the curry in a saucepan over low heat until warmed through, adding a splash of water or coconut milk to maintain a creamy consistency.

Anecdotes, Stories, and Quotes

Sri Lankan chef and author Peter Kuruvita has said, "Sri Lankan food is not just about taste and aroma; it is also about how it makes you feel." Plantain curry embodies this sentiment, offering a heartwarming and satisfying dish that showcases the flavors and traditions of Sri Lanka.

Chef Evaluation

Ala Kesel Muwa offers a perfect balance of flavors and textures, from the natural sweetness of plantains to the aromatic blend of spices. This curry provides a delicious and versatile addition to any Sri Lankan-inspired meal.

Serving Suggestions

Pair plantain curry with steamed rice or traditional Sri Lankan sides, such as string hoppers or roti, for an authentic and well-rounded dining experience.

Best Time to Eat

Enjoy Sri Lankan plantain curry as a flavorful and satisfying main course during lunch or dinner.

Conclusion

Experience the rich culinary traditions of Sri Lanka with this delightful plantain curry recipe. Relish the perfect balance of sweet plantains and fragrant spices in this versatile dish that brings the vibrant flavors of Sri Lanka to your table.

Plantain Rissoles - A Tropical Twist on a Classic

Introduction

Indulge in the delightful fusion of flavors with these plantain rissoles, a unique take on the traditional rissole recipe. Combining the sweet taste of ripe plantains with savory seasonings and a crispy exterior, these rissoles offer a tasty and innovative snack or appetizer for any occasion.

Brief History

Rissoles, a dish with roots in various cuisines, typically feature a filling of meat, seafood, or vegetables encased in a crispy coating. This recipe puts a tropical spin on the classic dish by incorporating plantains, showcasing the adaptability and versatility of this popular snack.

Ingredients

2 ripe plantains
1/2 cup breadcrumbs
1 egg
1/2 cup all-purpose flour
1 tsp garlic powder
1 tsp onion powder
Salt and pepper to taste
Oil for frying

Preparation Steps

Mash the ripe plantains until smooth.

Mix the mashed plantains with breadcrumbs, flour, garlic powder, onion powder, salt, and pepper until well combined.

Form the mixture into small, flattened patties.

Beat the egg in a small bowl.

Dip each plantain rissole in the beaten egg, ensuring they are evenly coated.

Heat oil in a heavy-bottomed pan or skillet over medium heat.

Fry the plantain rissoles for about 2-3 minutes on each side until golden brown and crispy.

Remove the cooked rissoles from the oil and place them on a paper towel-lined plate to drain any excess oil.

Serve the plantain rissoles warm with your choice of dipping sauces, such as spicy mayo or salsa.

Health Benefits
Plantains are a rich source of fiber, potassium, and vitamins, making these rissoles a nutritious snack or appetizer option. When enjoyed in moderation, they can contribute to a balanced and satisfying diet.

Storage and Reheating Information
Store leftover plantain rissoles in an airtight container in the refrigerator for up to 2 days. Reheat them in a preheated oven or toaster oven until heated through and crispy before serving.

Anecdotes, Stories, and Quotes
British-Jamaican chef and author Levi Roots once said, "Food is a great way to bring people together, and sharing dishes from different cultures helps us understand and appreciate one another." Plantain

rissoles epitomize this idea, merging diverse culinary influences into a single, delicious bite.

Chef Evaluation

Plantain rissoles provide a tasty and innovative twist on the classic rissole recipe. Their sweet and savory flavors, combined with a crispy exterior and soft interior, make them an ideal addition to any appetizer spread or snack platter.

Serving Suggestions

Enjoy plantain rissoles as a party appetizer or afternoon snack, serving them with a variety of dipping sauces to complement their unique flavor.

Best Time to Eat

Plantain rissoles can be enjoyed at any time of day, from a tasty midday snack to a flavorful addition to an evening gathering with friends and family.

Conclusion

Experience the delightful fusion of flavors and textures in these plantain rissoles, a unique and tasty twist on a classic dish. Indulge in the rich taste of ripe plantains and savory seasonings encased in a crispy coating for an unforgettable snack or appetizer.

Brazilian Plantain Chip Rolls (Roladinhos de Banana-da-Terra)

Introduction
Embark on a culinary journey to Brazil with these plantain chip rolls, a delectable finger food known as Roladinhos de Banana-da-Terra. This unique dish combines the crunchiness of plantain chips with the creaminess of cheese, offering a tantalizing array of textures and flavors that's perfect for snacking or serving at parties.

Brief History
Brazilian cuisine is known for its inventive use of local ingredients, including plantains. Roladinhos de Banana-da-Terra showcases the versatility of plantains in Brazilian cooking, resulting in a distinctive and delicious appetizer that highlights the country's rich culinary heritage.

Ingredients
20-25 plantain chips
1 cup cream cheese, softened
1/2 cup shredded mozzarella cheese
1/4 cup pitted olives, sliced
Salt and pepper to taste
Fresh parsley for garnish

Preparation Steps
Combine softened cream cheese, mozzarella cheese, salt, and pepper in a small bowl until well mixed.

Place a small amount of the cheese mixture on one end of a plantain chip.

Top the cheese mixture with a few sliced olives.

Roll the plantain chip into a tight cylinder, securing it with a toothpick if needed.

Repeat the process with the remaining chips, cheese mixture, and olives.

Arrange the plantain chip rolls on a serving platter and garnish with fresh parsley.

Serve chilled or at room temperature as a delightful appetizer or snack.

Health Benefits
Plantains are rich in fiber, potassium, and vitamins, offering various health benefits. These plantain chip rolls provide a nutritious and satisfying appetizer option when consumed in moderation.

Storage and Reheating Information
Store any leftover plantain chip rolls in an airtight container in the refrigerator for up to 2 days. These rolls are best enjoyed chilled or at room temperature, so no reheating is necessary.

Anecdotes, Stories, and Quotes
Brazilian chef and author Leticia Moreinos Schwartz once said, "Brazilian cuisine is all about using fresh, vibrant ingredients in creative ways." Plantain chip rolls are a perfect example of this, showcasing the innovative use of plantains in a unique and flavorful appetizer.

Chef Evaluation

Roladinhos de Banana-da-Terra offer a delightful balance of crunchy plantain chips and creamy cheese, with the added tanginess of olives. These distinctive rolls make for an impressive and tasty addition to any appetizer spread or party platter.

Serving Suggestions

Enjoy plantain chip rolls as an appetizer or party snack, pairing them with your favorite beverages or serving them alongside other small bites for a well-rounded spread.

Best Time to Eat

These plantain chip rolls are perfect for serving at social gatherings, such as parties or game nights, or as a delectable snack to enjoy at any time of day.

Conclusion

Experience the inventive flavors and textures of Brazilian cuisine with these plantain chip rolls. Delight in the unique combination of plantain chips, creamy cheese, and tangy olives for a memorable appetizer that's as delicious as it is visually appealing.

Jamaican Spicy Plantain Croquettes

Introduction
Experience the bold and vibrant flavors of Jamaica with these spicy plantain croquettes, a delicious snack that combines the sweetness of ripe plantains with a kick of spice. This unique dish offers a delightful balance of flavors and textures that will leave you craving more.

Brief History
Jamaican cuisine is known for its spicy and flavorful dishes that showcase the island's rich culinary heritage. Plantains, a staple ingredient in Caribbean cooking, are ingeniously transformed into these crispy croquettes for a tantalizing and authentic Jamaican snack.

Ingredients
2 ripe plantains
1/4 cup all-purpose flour
1/2 tsp baking powder
1/2 tsp salt
1/2 tsp ground black pepper
1/2 tsp cayenne pepper
1 egg
1/2 cup breadcrumbs
Oil for frying

Preparation Steps
Mash the ripe plantains until smooth.

Mix flour, baking powder, salt, black pepper, and cayenne pepper in a small bowl.

Add the flour mixture to the mashed plantains and mix well to combine.

Form the mixture into small, cylindrical croquettes.

Beat the egg in a small bowl.

Dip each croquette in the beaten egg, then roll in breadcrumbs until evenly coated.

Heat oil in a heavy-bottomed pan or skillet over medium heat.
Fry the croquettes for 2-3 minutes on each side until golden brown and crispy.

Remove the cooked croquettes from the oil and place them on a paper towel-lined plate to drain any excess oil.

Serve the spicy plantain croquettes warm with your choice of dipping sauces, such as jerk mayo or spicy ketchup.

Health Benefits
Plantains are a rich source of fiber, potassium, and vitamins, offering numerous health benefits. These spicy plantain croquettes provide a nutritious and satisfying snack option when enjoyed in moderation.

Storage and Reheating Information
Keep any remaining croquettes in an airtight container in the refrigerator for a maximum of 2 days. Reheat them in a preheated oven or toaster oven until heated through and crispy before serving.

Anecdotes, Stories, and Quotes
Jamaican chef and author Virginia Burke once said, "Jamaican food is a celebration of flavor and spice." Spicy plantain croquettes embody

this sentiment, showcasing the vibrant and bold flavors that make Jamaican cuisine so unique and beloved.

Chef Evaluation

These spicy plantain croquettes offer a delightful balance of sweet plantains and fiery spices, making for a memorable and tasty Jamaican-inspired snack. Their crispy exterior and soft interior create an irresistible textural contrast that's sure to impress.

Serving Suggestions

Enjoy these spicy plantain croquettes as an appetizer or party snack, pairing them with your favorite beverages or serving them alongside other Jamaican-inspired bites for a well-rounded spread.

Best Time to Eat

Spicy plantain croquettes are perfect for serving at social gatherings, such as parties or game nights, or as a delicious snack to enjoy at any time of day.

Conclusion

Immerse yourself in the bold and vibrant flavors of Jamaica with these spicy plantain croquettes. Delight in the harmonious balance of sweet plantains and fiery spices for a tasty and authentic Jamaican snack that's as delicious as it is unique.

Filipino Plantain Croquettes (Maruya)

Introduction
Dive into the rich flavors of the Philippines with these delectable plantain croquettes, known locally as Maruya. This delightful snack combines the natural sweetness of ripe plantains with a touch of sugar and a crispy coating, creating a delicious treat that's perfect for any occasion.

Brief History
Filipino cuisine is renowned for its inventive use of native ingredients, such as the versatile plantain. Maruya exemplifies this culinary tradition, showcasing the creative transformation of a simple ingredient into a mouthwatering snack enjoyed throughout the Philippines.

Ingredients
2 ripe plantains
1/4 cup brown sugar
1/2 cup all-purpose flour
1 egg
1 cup breadcrumbs
Oil for frying

Preparation Steps
Mash the ripe plantains until smooth and free of lumps.

Mix the brown sugar into the mashed plantains.

Gradually add flour to the plantain mixture, stirring to combine.
Form the mixture into small, flattened patties.

Beat the egg in a small bowl.

Dip each plantain patty in the beaten egg, then roll in breadcrumbs until fully coated.

Heat oil in a large, heavy-bottomed pan or skillet over medium heat.

Carefully place the croquettes in the hot oil, frying for 2-3 minutes on each side until golden brown and crispy.

Remove the cooked croquettes from the oil and place them on a paper towel-lined plate to drain excess oil.

Serve the plantain croquettes warm as a sweet and satisfying snack or dessert.

Health Benefits
Plantains are a good source of fiber, potassium, and essential vitamins, providing numerous health benefits. These plantain croquettes offer a healthier alternative to traditional desserts when enjoyed in moderation.

Storage and Reheating Information
Store leftover croquettes in an airtight container in the refrigerator for up to 2 days. Reheat them in a preheated oven or toaster oven until heated through and crispy before serving.

Anecdotes, Stories, and Quotes
Filipino chef and author Claude Tayag has said, "Filipino food is all about taking simple ingredients and transforming them into something extraordinary." Plantain croquettes exemplify this culinary philosophy, elevating a humble ingredient to create a delicious and beloved snack.

Chef Evaluation

These plantain croquettes strike a delightful balance between sweetness and crunch, making for a satisfying and tasty Filipino-inspired treat. Their crispy exterior and soft, sweet interior create an enticing textural contrast that's sure to impress.

Serving Suggestions

Enjoy these plantain croquettes as a dessert or sweet snack, pairing them with a hot cup of tea or coffee for a delightful mid-afternoon treat.

Best Time to Eat

Plantain croquettes are perfect for enjoying as a sweet indulgence at any time of day, whether as an after-dinner dessert or a mid-afternoon pick-me-up.

Conclusion

Experience the delightful flavors of the Philippines with these plantain croquettes, a unique and tasty snack that celebrates the essence of Filipino cuisine. Delight in the fusion of sweet plantains and a crispy coating for a unique and satisfying treat that's perfect for any occasion.

Argentinian Plantain Croquettes (Croquetas de Plátano)

Introduction

Embark on a culinary adventure to Argentina with these savory plantain croquettes, known as Croquetas de Plátano. Combining the sweetness of ripe plantains with the savoriness of cheese and spices, this unique dish offers a delightful fusion of flavors and textures that's perfect for any occasion.

Brief History

Argentinian cuisine is a melting pot of diverse culinary influences, resulting in a rich gastronomic landscape. Croquetas de Plátano exemplify this culinary creativity, showcasing the fusion of ingredients and flavors that make Argentinian cuisine so unique and enticing.

Ingredients

2 ripe plantains

1/2 cup shredded mozzarella cheese

1/4 cup all-purpose flour

1/2 tsp salt

1/2 tsp ground black pepper

1/4 tsp ground cumin

1 egg

1 cup breadcrumbs

Oil for frying

Preparation Steps

Mash the ripe plantains until smooth and free of lumps.

Mix shredded mozzarella cheese, flour, salt, black pepper, and ground cumin into the mashed plantains.

Form the mixture into small, cylindrical croquettes.

Beat the egg in a small bowl.

Dip each croquette in the beaten egg, then roll in breadcrumbs until fully coated.

Heat oil in a large, heavy-bottomed pan or skillet over medium heat.

Carefully place the croquettes in the hot oil, frying for 2-3 minutes on each side until golden brown and crispy.

Remove the cooked croquettes from the oil and place them on a paper towel-lined plate to drain excess oil.

Serve the plantain croquettes warm as a savory appetizer or snack.

Health Benefits
Plantains are rich in fiber, potassium, and essential vitamins, providing numerous health benefits. These plantain croquettes offer a more nutritious alternative to traditional fried snacks when enjoyed in moderation.

Storage and Reheating Information
Store leftover croquettes in an airtight container in the refrigerator for up to 2 days. Reheat them in a preheated oven or toaster oven until heated through and crispy before serving.

Anecdotes, Stories, and Quotes

Argentinian chef and author Francis Mallmann once said, "Argentinian cuisine is a reflection of the country's vibrant culture and history." Plantain croquettes encapsulate this sentiment, blending diverse flavors and ingredients to create a unique and delightful dish that's truly Argentinian.

Chef Evaluation

These plantain croquettes strike a perfect balance between sweet plantains and savory spices, resulting in a flavorful and satisfying Argentinian-inspired snack. Their crispy exterior and soft, cheesy interior create an enticing textural contrast that's sure to impress.

Serving Suggestions

Enjoy these plantain croquettes as an appetizer or party snack, pairing them with your favorite beverages or serving them alongside other Argentinian-inspired bites for a well-rounded spread.

Best Time to Eat

Plantain croquettes are perfect for serving at social gatherings, such as parties or game nights, or as a delicious snack to enjoy at any time of day.

Conclusion

Discover the diverse flavors and textures of Argentinian cuisine with these plantain croquettes, a unique and enticing snack that showcases the essence of this rich culinary tradition. Delight in the fusion of sweet plantains, savory spices, and creamy cheese for a memorable appetizer that's perfect for any occasion.

Vietnamese Sweet Plantain Dessert (Chuối Sứ Ở)

Introduction
Indulge in the sweet and comforting flavors of Vietnam with this plantain-based dessert called Chuối Sứ Ở. This delightful dish combines tender plantains with a rich coconut milk sauce, creating a harmonious blend of flavors that's sure to satisfy your sweet tooth.

Brief History
Vietnamese cuisine boasts a variety of sweet plantain dishes, with Chuối Sứ Ở being one of the most beloved. This traditional dessert showcases the delicate sweetness of plantains, simmered in a creamy sauce that embodies the essence of Vietnamese culinary traditions.

Ingredients
2 ripe plantains
1 cup coconut milk
1/4 cup palm sugar (or brown sugar)
1/2 tsp salt
1/2 tsp vanilla extract
1/4 tsp ground cinnamon
Optional toppings: toasted coconut flakes, sesame seeds, or crushed peanuts

Preparation Steps
Peel the plantains and slice them into 1-inch pieces.

In a medium saucepan, combine coconut milk, palm sugar, salt, vanilla extract, and ground cinnamon, whisking until well combined.

Bring the coconut milk mixture to a gentle simmer over medium heat, stirring occasionally.

Add the sliced plantains to the simmering coconut milk mixture, ensuring they're submerged.

Reduce heat to low and simmer for 15-20 minutes or until the plantains are tender and the sauce has thickened slightly.

Serve the sweet plantains warm with the rich coconut milk sauce and your choice of toppings, such as toasted coconut flakes, sesame seeds, or crushed peanuts.

Health Benefits
Plantains are a good source of fiber, potassium, and vitamins, offering numerous health benefits. This plantain dessert provides a healthier alternative to traditional sweets when enjoyed in moderation.

Storage and Reheating Information
Store any leftover plantain dessert in an airtight container in the refrigerator for up to 2 days. Reheat the dessert gently on the stovetop over low heat or in a microwave until warmed through before serving.

Anecdotes, Stories, and Quotes
Vietnamese-American chef and author Charles Phan once said, "Vietnamese cuisine is all about balance and harmony, blending flavors and textures to create something truly special." Chuối Sứ Ở exemplifies this philosophy, marrying sweet plantains and a rich coconut sauce to create a dessert that is uniquely Vietnamese.

Chef Evaluation
This plantain dessert strikes a perfect balance between sweet plantains and a rich coconut sauce, resulting in a delectable and comforting

Vietnamese sweet. Its tender plantains and aromatic sauce create an enticing symphony of flavors that's sure to impress.

Serving Suggestions
Enjoy this plantain dessert as a sweet treat after a meal or serve it as a delightful addition to a buffet-style gathering. Pair it with a hot cup of tea or coffee for the ultimate indulgence.

Best Time to Eat
Chuối Sứ Ở is perfect for serving after a meal or as a sweet afternoon pick-me-up. Enjoy it during special occasions or anytime you crave a sweet and comforting treat.

Conclusion
Delight in the sweet and aromatic flavors of Vietnam with this plantain dessert called Chuối Sứ Ở. Savor the harmonious combination of tender plantains and a rich coconut milk sauce for an exquisite and authentic Vietnamese sweet that's as satisfying as it is delicious.

Kenyan Plantain Banana Bread

Introduction
Experience the delightful fusion of East African flavors with this Kenyan Plantain Banana Bread, a creative twist on a beloved classic. Combining the natural sweetness of ripe plantains with traditional Kenyan spices, this wholesome treat offers a unique and delicious way to enjoy the essence of Kenyan culinary traditions.

Brief History
Kenyan cuisine incorporates a variety of fruits, grains, and spices in its diverse array of dishes. Plantain Banana Bread showcases the rich flavors of East Africa, bringing together ripe plantains, fragrant spices, and warm, inviting aromas to create an exceptional baked good that's perfect for any occasion.

Ingredients
2 ripe plantains
2 cups all-purpose flour
1 tsp baking soda
1/2 tsp salt
1 tsp ground cinnamon
1 tsp ground ginger
1/2 tsp ground nutmeg
1/2 cup unsalted butter, softened
1 cup brown sugar
2 eggs
1 tsp vanilla extract
Optional: 1/2 cup chopped walnuts or pecans

Preparation Steps

Preheat your oven to 350°F (180°C) and grease a 9x5 inch loaf pan.

Mash the ripe plantains until smooth and free of lumps.

In a separate medium-sized bowl, whisk together flour, baking soda, salt, cinnamon, ginger, and nutmeg.

In another bowl, blend softened butter and brown sugar until creamy and airy.

Beat eggs into the butter mixture one at a time, followed by vanilla extract.

Gradually incorporate the dry ingredients into the wet ingredients, mixing until just combined.

Fold mashed plantains (and optional chopped nuts) into the batter. Transfer the batter into the loaf pan and ensure the top is evenly smoothed.

Bake the plantain banana bread for 50-60 minutes or until a toothpick inserted into the center comes out clean.

Allow the bread to cool in the pan for 10 minutes, then remove it from the pan and let it cool completely on a wire rack.

Slice and serve your Kenyan Plantain Banana Bread with a warm cup of tea or coffee for a delightful and satisfying treat.

Health Benefits

Plantains offer various health benefits, including high fiber, potassium, and vitamin content. This plantain banana bread provides a healthier alternative to traditional baked goods when enjoyed in moderation.

Storage and Reheating Information

Store leftover banana bread in an airtight container at room temperature for up to 3 days or in the refrigerator for up to 1 week. Reheat individual slices in a toaster or oven until warmed through before serving.

Anecdotes, Stories, and Quotes

Kenyan chef and food writer Sheilla Kariuki has emphasized that "Kenyan cuisine celebrates local ingredients and rich flavors, resulting in unforgettable culinary experiences." Plantain Banana Bread perfectly encapsulates this sentiment, showcasing a distinctive blend of flavors that's uniquely Kenyan.

Chef Evaluation

This Plantain Banana Bread offers a delightful fusion of sweet plantains and fragrant spices, resulting in a warm and inviting treat that's perfect for any occasion. Its moist texture and aromatic flavors create a satisfying and delicious snack that's sure to impress.

Serving Suggestions

Enjoy this Plantain Banana Bread as a snack or breakfast treat, pairing it with your favorite spreads, such as butter, jam, or nut butter. It also makes a delightful addition to brunch or tea-time gatherings.

Best Time to Eat

Kenyan Plantain Banana Bread is perfect for enjoying at any time of day, whether as a breakfast treat, mid-afternoon snack, or after-dinner dessert.

Conclusion

Savor the rich and enticing flavors of East Africa with this Kenyan Plantain Banana Bread, a unique and delicious twist on a beloved classic. Delight in the fusion of sweet plantains and fragrant spices for a wholesome and satisfying treat that celebrates the essence of Kenyan culinary traditions.

Haitian Plantain Beignets (Banann Peze)

Introduction
Embark on a flavorful journey to Haiti with these plantain beignets, known as Banann Peze. Combining the sweetness of ripe plantains with the irresistible texture of fried dough, this traditional Haitian treat offers a delightful snack that's perfect for sharing with friends and family.

Brief History
Haitian cuisine boasts a rich and diverse culinary landscape, with plantains playing a prominent role in many dishes. Banann Peze showcases the versatility of plantains, transforming them into a crispy, golden-fried delight that's been enjoyed for generations.

Ingredients
2 ripe plantains
1/2 cup all-purpose flour
1 tsp baking powder
1/4 tsp salt
1 tbsp sugar
1/2 cup water
Oil for frying
Optional toppings: powdered sugar, cinnamon sugar, or honey

Preparation Steps
Mash the ripe plantains until smooth and free of lumps.

Combine flour, baking powder, salt, and sugar in a medium-sized bowl.

Gradually whisk in water to form a smooth, pancake-like batter.

Fold mashed plantains into the batter until well combined.

Heat oil in a large, heavy-bottomed pan or skillet over medium heat.

Carefully drop spoonfuls of batter into the hot oil, frying for 2-3 minutes on each side until golden brown and crispy.

Remove cooked beignets from the oil and place them on a paper towel-lined plate to drain excess oil.

Sprinkle with your choice of toppings, such as powdered sugar, cinnamon sugar, or a drizzle of honey, before serving.

Health Benefits

Plantains are rich in fiber, potassium, and essential vitamins, offering numerous health benefits. These plantain beignets provide a more nutritious alternative to traditional fried snacks when enjoyed in moderation.

Storage and Reheating Information

Plantain beignets are best enjoyed fresh and hot, as they may lose their crispy texture over time. If needed, store leftovers in an airtight container at room temperature and reheat them in a preheated oven or toaster oven until warmed through and crispy before serving.

Anecdotes, Stories, and Quotes

Haitian-American chef and cookbook author Cindy Similien has emphasized that "Haitian cuisine is a vibrant tapestry of flavors and traditions, reflecting the rich history of the island." Plantain beignets perfectly embody this sentiment, showcasing the creative use of local ingredients and flavors in a delightful snack.

Chef Evaluation

These Haitian plantain beignets strike a perfect balance between sweetness and texture, resulting in a delectable snack that's perfect for any occasion. Their crispy exterior and soft, tender interior create an enticing contrast that's sure to satisfy.

Serving Suggestions

Enjoy these plantain beignets as a sweet snack or dessert, pairing them with your favorite beverages or serving them alongside other Haitian-inspired bites for a well-rounded culinary experience.

Best Time to Eat

Haitian plantain beignets are perfect for enjoying as an afternoon snack or after-dinner treat, alongside a cup of coffee or your favorite warm beverage.

Conclusion

Discover the rich and enticing flavors of Haiti with these plantain beignets, a delectable and traditional snack that showcases the best of the island's culinary traditions. Delight in the perfect balance of sweet plantains and crispy fried dough for a truly unforgettable treat.

Jamaican Fried Green Plantains (Tostones)

Introduction

Indulge in the flavors of the Caribbean with Jamaican-style fried green plantains, known as Tostones. This delectable side dish showcases the versatility of plantains, combining their mildly sweet flavor with a crispy, golden crust for a unique and satisfying accompaniment to any meal.

Brief History

Fried green plantains are a beloved staple in Jamaican cuisine, highlighting the influence of various culinary traditions on the island's food culture. Tostones offer a delicious and simple way to enjoy the natural flavors of plantains while adding a satisfying crunch to your plate.

Ingredients

2 green plantains
Kosher salt (or your preferred seasoning)
Oil for frying
Optional dipping sauce: Jamaican Jerk Sauce or garlic aioli

Preparation Steps

Slice the ends off the plantains and make a shallow slit down the side to peel off the skin.

Cut the plantains into 1-inch thick slices on a diagonal angle.

Heat oil in a large, heavy-bottomed skillet or frying pan over medium-high heat.

Fry the plantain slices for 2-3 minutes on each side or until golden and lightly crisp.

Remove the fried plantain slices from the oil and place them on a paper towel-lined plate to drain excess oil.

Lightly flatten the fried plantain slices using a tostonera, plantain press, or the flat bottom of a glass.

Return the flattened plantains to the hot oil, frying them for an additional 1-2 minutes on each side until golden brown and crispy.

Take out the fried plantains from the oil and transfer them to a plate lined with paper towels to absorb any extra oil.

Sprinkle the tostones with kosher salt or your preferred seasoning before serving alongside your favorite dipping sauce.

Health Benefits
Green plantains offer various health benefits, including high fiber content and essential vitamins and minerals. Tostones provide a delicious and more nutritious alternative to traditional potato-based side dishes when enjoyed in moderation.

Storage and Reheating Information
Fried green plantains are best enjoyed fresh and hot, as they may lose their crispy texture over time. If needed, store leftovers in an airtight container in the refrigerator and reheat them in a preheated oven or toaster oven until warmed through and crispy before serving.

Anecdotes, Stories, and Quotes
Jamaican chef and food writer Grace Barrington-Shaw once stated that "Jamaican cuisine is an embodiment of the island's vibrant

history and diverse cultural influences." Tostones exemplify this idea, showcasing a simple yet delicious way to enjoy plantains that reflects Jamaica's rich culinary traditions.

Chef Evaluation

Jamaican Fried Green Plantains strike a perfect balance between mild sweetness and a crispy, golden crust, resulting in an enticing side dish that complements any meal. Their unique flavor and texture make them a satisfying addition to your culinary repertoire.

Serving Suggestions

Enjoy these fried green plantains as a side dish alongside Jamaican-inspired main courses or your favorite proteins, such as jerk chicken or grilled shrimp. Pair them with a savory dipping sauce like Jamaican Jerk Sauce or garlic aioli for added flavor.

Best Time to Eat

Tostones are perfect for enjoying as a side dish at any meal, from casual weeknight dinners to lively weekend gatherings with friends and family.

Conclusion

Discover the vibrant flavors of Jamaica with these Fried Green Plantains, a delectable side dish that highlights the best of the island's culinary traditions. Delight in their unique taste and texture for a satisfying and memorable addition to any meal.

Indonesian Fried Plantain Waffles (Wafel Pisang Goreng)

Introduction
Embark on a flavorful journey to Indonesia with these Fried Plantain Waffles, known as Wafel Pisang Goreng. Combining the natural sweetness of ripe plantains with the irresistible texture of crispy waffles, this unique Indonesian treat offers a delightful and innovative twist on traditional waffles that's perfect for any occasion.

Brief History
Indonesian cuisine is rich in its variety and fusion of flavors. Wafel Pisang Goreng showcases the creative use of plantains in this diverse culinary landscape, bringing together ripe plantains, fragrant spices, and warm, inviting aromas to create a tantalizing snack that reflects the essence of Indonesian food culture.

Ingredients
2 ripe plantains
1 1/2 cups all-purpose flour
1 tbsp baking powder
1/2 tsp salt
1 tsp ground cinnamon
1/4 tsp ground nutmeg
1/4 cup sugar
2 eggs
1 cup whole milk
2 tbsp unsalted butter, melted
Oil for frying
Optional toppings: whipped cream, fresh fruit, maple syrup

Preparation Steps

Mash the ripe plantains until smooth and free of lumps.

In a large bowl, mix flour, baking powder, salt, cinnamon, nutmeg, and sugar.

In a different bowl, whisk eggs, milk, and melted butter until well combined.

Blend the wet and dry ingredients together, stirring until just mixed.

Fold mashed plantains into the batter until well incorporated.

Heat your waffle iron according to the manufacturer's instructions and lightly grease with oil or cooking spray.

Spoon the batter onto the heated waffle iron and cook until golden brown and crispy on the outside.

Remove the cooked waffle from the iron and place it on a paper towel-lined plate to drain any excess oil.

Repeat with the remaining batter.

Serve your Indonesian Fried Plantain Waffles warm, topped with whipped cream, fresh fruit, and a drizzle of maple syrup.

Health Benefits

Plantains offer various health benefits, including high fiber content, potassium, and essential vitamins. These waffles provide a more nutritious alternative to traditional waffles when enjoyed in moderation.

Storage and Reheating Information

Store leftover waffles in an airtight container in the refrigerator for up to 2-3 days. Reheat in a toaster or oven until warmed through and crispy before serving.

Anecdotes, Stories, and Quotes

Indonesian culinary expert and cookbook author Sri Owen has shared that "Indonesian cuisine is a symphony of flavors and spices, reflecting the country's diverse history and culture." Fried Plantain Waffles exemplify this idea, blending the natural sweetness of plantains with aromatic spices to create an enticing snack.

Chef Evaluation

These Indonesian Fried Plantain Waffles offer a delightful fusion of sweet plantains and fragrant spices, resulting in a warm and inviting treat that's perfect for any occasion. Their crispy exterior and tender interior create a satisfying contrast that's sure to impress.

Serving Suggestions

Enjoy these plantain waffles for breakfast or brunch, pairing them with savory breakfast proteins, such as eggs or bacon. They also make a delightful dessert when topped with ice cream, fresh fruit, and chocolate sauce.

Best Time to Eat

Wafel Pisang Goreng can be enjoyed at any time of day, whether as a sweet breakfast treat or an indulgent dessert after a savory Indonesian-inspired meal.

Conclusion

Experience the enticing flavors of Indonesia with these Fried Plantain Waffles, a unique and delicious twist on traditional waffles. Delight in the fusion of sweet plantains and aromatic spices for a wholesome and satisfying treat that celebrates the essence of Indonesian culinary traditions.

Costa Rican-Style Fried Plantains
(Patacones)

Introduction
Indulge in the flavors of Central America with these Costa Rican-style fried plantains, known as Patacones. Combining the subtle sweetness of ripe plantains with a crispy, golden crust, this traditional Costa Rican side dish offers a delightful accompaniment to any meal, showcasing the versatility of plantains in this vibrant culinary culture.

Brief History
Costa Rican cuisine is rich in its fusion of flavors and traditions. Patacones exemplify the innovative use of plantains in this culinary landscape, bringing forth a crispy, golden-fried treat that has been enjoyed throughout generations.

Ingredients
2 green plantains
Kosher salt (or your preferred seasoning)
Oil for frying
Optional dipping sauce: Salsa Lizano or cilantro-lime crema

Preparation Steps
Slice the ends off the plantains and make a shallow slit down the side to peel off the skin.

Cut the plantains into 1-inch thick slices on a diagonal angle.

Heat oil in a large, heavy-bottomed skillet or frying pan over medium-high heat.

Fry the plantain slices for 2-3 minutes on each side or until golden and lightly crisp.

Take out the fried plantain slices from the oil and transfer them to a plate lined with paper towels to absorb any excess oil.

Lightly flatten the fried plantain slices using a tostonera, plantain press, or the flat bottom of a glass.

Return the flattened plantains to the hot oil, frying them for an additional 1-2 minutes on each side until golden brown and crispy.

Remove the fried plantains from the oil and place them on a paper towel-lined plate to drain excess oil.

Sprinkle the patacones with kosher salt or your preferred seasoning before serving alongside your favorite dipping sauce.

Health Benefits

Green plantains offer numerous health benefits, including high fiber content, potassium, and essential vitamins. Patacones provide a more nutritious alternative to traditional fried snacks when enjoyed in moderation.

Storage and Reheating Information

Patacones are best enjoyed fresh and hot, as they may lose their crispy texture over time. If needed, store leftovers in an airtight container in the refrigerator and reheat them in a preheated oven or toaster oven until warmed through and crispy before serving.

Anecdotes, Stories, and Quotes

Costa Rican chef and culinary instructor, Isabel Campabadal, has emphasized that "Costa Rican cuisine is an expression of the country's rich history, biodiversity, and cultural influences." Patacones showcase this idea, celebrating the traditional use of plantains in a simple yet enticing dish.

Chef Evaluation

These Costa Rican-Style Fried Plantains strike a perfect balance between subtle sweetness and a crispy, golden crust, resulting in a versatile side dish that complements any meal. Their unique flavor and texture make them a satisfying addition to your culinary repertoire.

Serving Suggestions

Enjoy these patacones as a side dish alongside traditional Costa Rican-inspired meals, such as Gallo Pinto or Casados. Pair them with flavorful dipping sauces like Salsa Lizano or cilantro-lime crema for added zest.

Best Time to Eat

Patacones can be enjoyed at any time of day, whether as a savory breakfast side dish or a delicious accompaniment to a lunch or dinner meal.

Conclusion

Embrace the enticing flavors of Costa Rica with these Fried Plantains, a delectable side dish that celebrates the best of this Central American nation's culinary traditions. Delight in the fusion of crispy, golden plantains with aromatic spices for a satisfying treat that adds depth and texture to any meal.

Ugandan Plantain Cassava Fufu

Introduction
Delve into the rich and flavorful world of Ugandan cuisine with this Plantain Cassava Fufu recipe. A harmonious blend of plantains and cassava, this hearty side dish offers a unique and satisfying accompaniment to any meal, celebrating the essence of Ugandan food culture.

Brief History
Ugandan cuisine is characterized by its diverse ingredients and culinary influences. Plantain Cassava Fufu showcases the creative use of starchy staples, such as plantains and cassava, resulting in a filling and delicious dish that has been enjoyed throughout generations.

Ingredients
2 ripe plantains
1 lb cassava root, peeled and cut into small pieces
Water
Kosher salt (or your preferred seasoning)
Optional: butter or margarine for added richness

Preparation Steps
Peel the plantains and cassava, and cut them into small pieces.

In a sizable pot, bring water to a boil and add salt according to your taste.

Add the plantain and cassava pieces to the boiling water and cook until both ingredients are soft and easily mashed, approximately 20-25 minutes.

Drain the excess water, reserving some for adjusting the fufu consistency later, if needed.

Using a potato masher or mortar and pestle, mash the cooked plantain and cassava into a smooth, thick paste. Add butter or margarine for added richness if desired.

If the fufu is too thick, gradually add the reserved water until the desired consistency is achieved. If too thin, return the mixture to low heat and stir constantly until thickened.

Taste and adjust seasoning as needed before serving your Ugandan Plantain Cassava Fufu alongside your favorite stews, soups, or sauces.

Health Benefits
Plantains and cassava offer a variety of health benefits, including high fiber content, potassium, and essential vitamins. When consumed in moderation, this dish serves as a nutritious and filling side dish.

Storage and Reheating Information
Ugandan Plantain Cassava Fufu is best enjoyed fresh and warm. If needed, store leftovers in an airtight container in the refrigerator and reheat in a microwave-safe dish until warmed through before serving.

Anecdotes, Stories, and Quotes
Ugandan chef and food writer, Sylvia Nalubwama, has emphasized that "Ugandan food culture is a celebration of locally-sourced ingredients and time-honored cooking techniques." Plantain Cassava Fufu encapsulates this sentiment, showcasing a delicious fusion of starchy staples that has been cherished for generations.

Chef Evaluation

This Ugandan Plantain Cassava Fufu recipe artfully blends the natural sweetness of plantains with the earthy flavor of cassava, resulting in a hearty and satisfying side dish that complements a variety of main courses.

Serving Suggestions

Enjoy this plantain cassava fufu alongside traditional Ugandan stews, such as groundnut stew or beef stew, allowing the flavors to meld for an authentic culinary experience.

Best Time to Eat

Plantain Cassava Fufu is typically enjoyed as a filling side dish during lunch or dinner, often accompanying rich stews or soups for a balanced meal.

Conclusion

Embark on a culinary adventure to Uganda with this Plantain Cassava Fufu recipe, a delightful and hearty side dish that pays homage to the rich culinary traditions of this East African nation. Relish in the comforting flavors and inviting textures as you savor this authentic taste of Uganda.

South Indian Plantain Cassava Dosa

Introduction
Experience the vibrant flavors of South India with this Plantain Cassava Dosa recipe. This unique twist on the traditional dosa combines the earthy sweetness of plantains and cassava with the tanginess of fermented batter, resulting in a crispy, golden crepe that's perfect for any time of day.

Brief History
South Indian cuisine is known for its diverse and flavorful dishes, with dosas being a beloved staple. Plantain Cassava Dosa presents an innovative fusion of starchy staples, reflecting the culinary ingenuity and adaptability of South Indian food culture.

Ingredients
1 cup uncooked rice
1/2 cup uncooked urad dal (split, skinned black lentils)
1/4 cup uncooked cassava root, grated
1 ripe plantain, peeled and chopped
2 tbsp fenugreek seeds
Vegetable oil for cooking
Salt to taste

Preparation Steps
Soak rice, urad dal, and fenugreek seeds separately in water for 4-6 hours.

Drain the water from the rice and dal, then grind them separately into smooth pastes using a wet grinder or food processor, adding water as needed.

Combine the rice and dal pastes in a large bowl and mix well. Add salt to taste.

Cover and let the batter ferment for 8-10 hours at room temperature or overnight. The batter should double in volume and have a slightly sour aroma.

Mash the ripe plantain and grated cassava, then mix them into the fermented batter.

Heat a flat non-stick pan or dosa tawa over medium-high heat and lightly grease with oil.

Pour a ladleful of batter into the center of the pan and quickly spread it in a circular motion to form a thin, even layer.

Drizzle oil around the edges of the dosa and let it cook until the underside is golden brown.

Carefully flip the dosa and cook the other side until crisp and golden.

Fold the dosa in half or into a cone shape and serve hot with your favorite chutneys and sambar.

Health Benefits
Plantains, cassava, and fermented batter provide a variety of nutrients, such as fiber, potassium, and essential vitamins. When consumed in moderation, this dish serves as a wholesome and nutritious meal option.

Storage and Reheating Information
Dosas are best enjoyed fresh and hot. If necessary, store any leftover batter in an airtight container in the refrigerator for a maximum of 2

days. Before making dosas, allow the refrigerated batter to reach room temperature.

Anecdotes, Stories, and Quotes
Acclaimed South Indian chef, Suresh Pillai, emphasizes that "South Indian cuisine is a symphony of flavors and textures, showcasing the region's passion for innovation and adaptability." Plantain Cassava Dosa exemplifies this spirit, combining traditional ingredients in a delightfully inventive way.

Chef Evaluation
This South Indian Plantain Cassava Dosa recipe harmoniously blends the earthy sweetness of plantains and cassava with the tanginess of fermented batter, resulting in a delicately crisp crepe that's sure to impress.

Serving Suggestions
Serve this plantain cassava dosa alongside an array of South Indian chutneys and sambar for a satisfying meal. Enjoy it for breakfast, lunch, or dinner, as it's versatile and filling.

Best Time to Eat
Dosas can be enjoyed at any time of day, but they're especially popular as a breakfast item or a light, satisfying meal option throughout the day.

Conclusion
Experience the dynamic flavors of South India with this Plantain Cassava Dosa recipe, a delightful fusion of ingredients that celebrates the culinary ingenuity and adaptability of this vibrant region. Relish the unique combination of textures and flavors as you savor this delicious twist on a traditional dosa.

Nigerian Plantain Eba (Amala Ogede)

Introduction
Indulge in the bold flavors of Nigeria with this Plantain Eba, also known as Amala Ogede. This traditional swallow dish boasts a soft, moldable texture and subtle sweetness, offering a delightful accompaniment to various soups and stews that showcase the heart of Nigerian cuisine.

Brief History
Nigerian cuisine is rich in its fusion of flavors and cultural influences. Plantain Eba highlights the versatility of plantains in this culinary landscape, providing a unique and satisfying alternative to traditional yam or cassava-based swallows.

Ingredients
2 green plantains
Water for boiling
Optionally, consider adding spinach or other leafy greens for additional nutrition.
Kosher salt (or your preferred seasoning)

Preparation Steps
Peel and chop the green plantains into small pieces.

In a sizable pot, bring water to a boil and season with salt to your preference.

Add the plantain pieces to the boiling water and cook for 15-20 minutes or until soft and tender.

Drain the water from the cooked plantains and mash them into a smooth paste using a potato masher or mortar and pestle.

If desired, add spinach or other leafy greens to the plantain mixture for added nutrition.

Stir the mixture until the plantains and greens are evenly combined.

Form small, golf-sized balls of the plantain eba mixture and serve alongside your favorite Nigerian soups or stews.

Health Benefits
Plantains offer numerous health benefits, including high fiber content, potassium, and essential vitamins. Amala Ogede provides a nutritious and filling side dish when enjoyed in moderation.

Storage and Reheating Information
Plantain Eba is best enjoyed fresh and hot. If needed, store leftovers in an airtight container in the refrigerator and reheat in a microwave-safe dish until warmed through before serving.

Anecdotes, Stories, and Quotes
Nigerian chef and food blogger, Adeola Adegoke, has emphasized that "Nigerian cuisine is a celebration of bold flavors and versatile ingredients." Plantain Eba highlights this concept, showcasing the ingenuity of transforming plantains into a unique and delightful dish.

Chef Evaluation
This Nigerian Plantain Eba recipe presents a soft, moldable texture and subtle sweetness, creating a versatile side dish that beautifully complements the rich flavors of Nigerian soups and stews.

Serving Suggestions

Serve this plantain eba alongside traditional Nigerian soups and stews like Egusi, Okra, or Efo Riro for an authentic and delicious meal.

Best Time to Eat

Plantain Eba can be enjoyed at any time of day, often accompanying flavorful soups or stews for a filling lunch or dinner.

Conclusion

Embark on a culinary adventure to Nigeria with this Plantain Eba recipe, a delightful side dish that celebrates the essence of Nigerian cuisine. Experience the versatility of plantains as you savor the subtle sweetness and soft texture of Amala Ogede paired with a variety of rich and flavorful soups or stews.

Portuguese Plantain Fries (Batatas Fritas de Platano)

Introduction

Experience a taste of Portugal with these delectable Plantain Fries, known as Batatas Fritas de Platano. Crisp on the outside and tender within, this delightful twist on traditional french fries highlights the sweet, satisfying flavor of plantains, offering a versatile snack or side dish that's perfect for any occasion.

Brief History

Portuguese cuisine showcases a fusion of Mediterranean and Atlantic influences, with a focus on fresh ingredients and flavors. Plantain Fries embody this culinary spirit, presenting a unique take on a beloved classic that celebrates the versatility of plantains.

Ingredients

2 ripe plantains
2 tbsp olive oil
1 tsp smoked paprika
1 tsp garlic powder
1 tsp onion powder
1/2 tsp ground cumin
Season with kosher salt and freshly ground black pepper according to your taste.
Garnish with finely chopped fresh cilantro or parsley.

Preparation Steps

Preheat the oven to 425°F (220°C) and cover a baking sheet with parchment paper.

Peel the plantains and cut them into fry-shaped pieces, about 1/2-inch thick.

In a large mixing bowl, combine olive oil, smoked paprika, garlic powder, onion powder, and ground cumin.

Add the plantain pieces to the seasoning mixture and gently toss to coat them evenly.

Arrange the plantain fries in a single layer on the prepared baking sheet.

Bake in the preheated oven for 20-25 minutes or until golden brown and crispy, flipping them halfway through the cooking time.

Once cooked, remove the plantain fries from the oven and season with salt and pepper to taste.

Garnish with freshly chopped cilantro or parsley before serving your Portuguese Plantain Fries alongside your favorite dipping sauce or main dish.

Health Benefits

Plantains offer numerous health benefits, including high fiber content, potassium, and essential vitamins. These baked plantain fries provide a healthier alternative to traditional fried snacks when enjoyed in moderation.

Storage and Reheating Informationn

Plantain Fries are best enjoyed fresh and hot. If needed, store leftovers in an airtight container in the refrigerator and reheat in a preheated 425°F (220°C) oven until warmed through and crispy.

Anecdotes, Stories, and Quotes

Renowned Portuguese chef, José Avillez, has emphasized the significance of embracing tradition while exploring new flavors: "Portuguese cuisine is a reflection of our history, yet it's constantly evolving with innovative ingredients and techniques." Plantain Fries encapsulate this idea, offering a delicious and inventive twist on a classic favorite.

Chef Evaluation

These Portuguese Plantain Fries deliver a delightful balance of sweet and savory flavors with a satisfyingly crispy texture. Perfect as a snack or side dish, they serve as a versatile and delectable treat for any occasion.

Serving Suggestions

Savor these plantain fries alongside Portuguese dishes like Piri-Piri Chicken or Bacalhau à Brás for an authentic culinary experience. Experiment with various dipping sauces, such as spicy mayo or garlicky aioli, to create your perfect flavor combination.

Best Time to Eat

Plantain Fries can be enjoyed at any time of day, whether as a satisfying snack or a flavorful side dish for lunch or dinner.

Conclusion

Experience the essence of Portuguese cuisine with these Plantain Fries, a delightful and inventive twist on a beloved classic. Relish in the sweet and savory flavors, along with the crispy, golden texture as you savor Batatas Fritas de Platano paired with your favorite sauces or dishes for an authentic taste of Portugal.

Canadian Plantain Poutine

Introduction

Discover the flavors of Canada with this unique Plantain Poutine recipe. This tasty twist on a classic Canadian dish combines crispy plantain fries with rich gravy and creamy cheese curds, offering a delightful fusion of sweet and savory flavors that's perfect for sharing with friends and family.

Brief History

Poutine, a quintessential Canadian dish, originated in Quebec in the late 1950s. Over time, it has evolved to include various ingredients and toppings. Plantain Poutine celebrates the traditional elements of this beloved comfort food while incorporating the sweet and hearty flavor of plantains.

Ingredients

2 ripe plantains
2 tbsp olive oil
1/2 cup cheese curds
1/4 cup beef or vegetable gravy (store-bought or homemade)
Freshly ground black pepper, to taste
Chopped fresh parsley or chives, for garnish

Preparation Steps

Preheat the oven to 425°F (220°C) and prepare a baking sheet by lining it with parchment paper.

Peel the plantains and cut them into fry-shaped pieces, about 1/2-inch thick.

Toss the plantain pieces with olive oil and spread them in a single layer on the prepared baking sheet.

Bake in the preheated oven for 20-25 minutes or until golden brown and crispy, flipping them halfway through the cooking time.

Remove the plantain fries from the oven and transfer them to a serving dish.

Sprinkle the cheese curds over the hot plantain fries, allowing them to melt slightly.

Drizzle the warm gravy on top of the cheese curds and plantain fries.

Add freshly ground black pepper to taste and garnish with chopped fresh parsley or chives.

Serve your Canadian Plantain Poutine immediately to enjoy the ultimate combination of textures and flavors.

Health Benefits
Plantains are a good source of fiber, potassium, and essential vitamins. When consumed in moderation, this Plantain Poutine can be part of a balanced diet and a delightful way to indulge in Canadian cuisine.

Storage and Reheating Information
Plantain Poutine is best enjoyed fresh and hot, as reheating may compromise the dish's texture. If needed, store the plantain fries, gravy, and cheese curds separately in airtight containers in the refrigerator and assemble when ready to serve.

Anecdotes, Stories, and Quotes

Renowned Canadian chef, Massimo Capra, once said, "Food is all about culture, and it's important to stay true to your roots while exploring new flavors and ingredients." Plantain Poutine embodies this sentiment, combining traditional elements of Canadian cuisine with the sweet and hearty flavor of plantains.

Chef Evaluation

This Canadian Plantain Poutine delivers a delicious fusion of textures and flavors, from crispy plantain fries to creamy cheese curds and savory gravy. It serves as a versatile and satisfying dish perfect for sharing with loved ones or as a comforting indulgence.

Serving Suggestions

Enjoy this Plantain Poutine alongside other Canadian-inspired dishes, such as Montreal-style smoked meat or butter tarts, for an authentic taste of the country's diverse cuisine. Pair with a crisp Canadian lager or a glass of Niagara wine for a well-rounded dining experience.

Best Time to Eat

Plantain Poutine can be enjoyed at any time of day, whether as a hearty lunch, a comforting dinner, or a late-night snack after exploring the bustling cities and picturesque landscapes of Canada.

Conclusion

Experience the heart of Canadian cuisine with this Plantain Poutine recipe, a delightful twist on a classic dish. Embrace the fusion of sweet and savory flavors as you indulge in crispy plantain fries, rich gravy, and creamy cheese curds, transporting your taste buds on a journey through the diverse culinary landscape of Canada.

Japanese Plantain Tempura

Introduction

Embark on a culinary journey to Japan with this Plantain Tempura recipe. This unique twist on traditional tempura showcases the sweet, delicious flavor of plantains, wrapped in a delicate, crispy batter. Perfect as a snack or appetizer, Plantain Tempura introduces a delightful fusion of flavors that will leave you craving more.

Brief History

Tempura, a beloved Japanese dish, has its roots in Portuguese cuisine, introduced to Japan in the 16th century. Over time, it has evolved to become a quintessential part of Japanese culinary culture. Plantain Tempura combines the traditional tempura technique with the sweet and hearty flavor of plantains, resulting in a delightful and innovative creation.

Ingredients

2 ripe plantains
1 cup all-purpose flour
1/4 cup cornstarch
1/2 tsp baking powder
1/2 tsp kosher salt
1 cup ice-cold sparkling water
Vegetable or canola oil, for frying
Kosher salt, for seasoning
Tempura dipping sauce or your preferred dipping sauce

Preparation Steps

Prepare the tempura batter by mixing the all-purpose flour, cornstarch, baking powder, and salt in a large mixing bowl.

Slowly pour the ice-cold sparkling water into the dry ingredients and gently whisk until just combined. Be careful not to overmix, as lumps in the batter are desired.

Peel and slice the plantains into thin, 1/4-inch thick slices.

In a deep, heavy-bottomed pot or deep fryer, heat the oil to 350°F (175°C).

Dip each plantain slice into the tempura batter, ensuring they are fully coated, and carefully place them in the hot oil.

Fry the plantain tempura for 2-3 minutes or until golden brown and crispy.

Remove the cooked tempura from the oil and transfer to a wire rack or paper towel-lined plate to drain any excess oil.

Sprinkle a pinch of kosher salt over the dish while it's still hot.

Serve your Japanese Plantain Tempura immediately with your favorite tempura dipping sauce or another sauce of your choice.

Health Benefits
Plantains are a good source of fiber, potassium, and essential vitamins. When consumed in moderation, this Plantain Tempura can be part of a balanced diet and an enjoyable way to experience Japanese cuisine.

Storage and Reheating Information
Plantain Tempura is best enjoyed fresh and hot, as reheating may compromise the dish's texture. If needed, store leftovers in an airtight container in the refrigerator and reheat in a preheated 375°F (190°C) oven until warmed through and crispy.

Anecdotes, Stories, and Quotes

Renowned Japanese chef, Masaharu Morimoto, has said, "Tempura is a delicate balance of texture and flavor that highlights the beauty of simplicity in Japanese cuisine." Plantain Tempura showcases this balance, combining the sweet and hearty flavor of plantains with a light, crispy batter for a delightful fusion of cultures.

Chef Evaluation

This Japanese Plantain Tempura recipe delivers a delectable fusion of flavors and textures, from the sweet plantains to the delicate, crispy batter. It serves as a versatile and enticing appetizer that's perfect for sharing with friends or enjoying as a satisfying snack.

Serving Suggestions

Savor this Plantain Tempura alongside other Japanese-inspired dishes, such as vegetable gyoza or miso soup, for a well-rounded meal. Pair with a crisp, refreshing lager or green tea to balance the flavors and textures.

Best Time to Eat

Plantain Tempura can be enjoyed at any time of day, whether as a flavorful appetizer before your main meal or a satisfying afternoon snack.

Conclusion

Experience the essence of Japanese cuisine with this Plantain Tempura recipe, a unique twist on a beloved dish. Indulge in the delicious fusion of sweet plantains and delicate, crispy batter as you savor the flavors of Japan in each delightful bite.

Puerto Rican Fried Green Plantain Pies
(Pastelillos de Plátano Verde)

Introduction
Discover the vibrant flavors of Puerto Rico with these savory Green Plantain Pies, known as Pastelillos de Plátano Verde. Combining starchy green plantains, seasoned ground beef, and flavorful sofrito, this traditional street food offers a delicious and authentic taste of Puerto Rican cuisine.

Brief History
Pastelillos de Plátano Verde have been a beloved staple of Puerto Rican cuisine for generations. Influenced by the island's diverse culinary history, these fried green plantain pies showcase the unique blend of flavors and ingredients that make Puerto Rican food so distinctive.

Ingredients
4 green plantains
2 tbsp olive oil
1 lb (450g) ground beef
1/2 cup sofrito (store-bought or homemade)
1 tbsp tomato sauce
1 tsp kosher salt
1 tsp ground black pepper
Vegetable oil, for frying
Optional toppings: shredded lettuce, diced tomato, sliced avocado, hot sauce, or mayo-ketchup

Preparation Steps

Peel the green plantains and cut them into large chunks. Soak the plantain pieces in salted water for 30 minutes.

While that's happening, warm olive oil in a large skillet over medium heat. Add ground beef and cook until browned, breaking it apart with a wooden spoon.

Stir in sofrito, tomato sauce, salt, and pepper, and cook for an additional 5 minutes, allowing flavors to meld. Remove the beef mixture from heat and set aside.

Remove the plantain pieces from the salted water and pat dry with a paper towel.

Use a tostonera (plantain press) or a flat object, such as a cutting board, to flatten the plantain chunks into thin discs.

Fill a deep, heavy-bottomed pot or deep fryer with vegetable oil and heat it to 350°F (175°C).

Fry the flattened plantain discs until golden and crispy on both sides, about 3-4 minutes. Take out from the oil and let it drain on a plate lined with paper towels.

To assemble, place a heaping spoonful of the ground beef mixture onto a fried plantain disc and fold it in half, creating a semi-circle-shaped pie.

Use kitchen twine or toothpicks to secure the plantain pies and return them to the hot oil, frying until the filling is heated through and the plantain exterior is crispy, about 2-3 minutes.

Serve your Puerto Rican Fried Green Plantain Pies with your choice of toppings and a side of hot sauce or mayo-ketchup for a truly authentic experience.

Health Benefits

Green plantains offer fiber, potassium, and essential vitamins. When consumed in moderation, these plantain pies can be a delicious addition to a balanced diet and a great way to explore Puerto Rican cuisine.

Storage and Reheating Information

Pastelillos de Plátano Verde are best enjoyed fresh and hot. If needed, store leftovers in an airtight container in the refrigerator and reheat in a preheated 375°F (190°C) oven until warmed through and crispy.

Anecdotes, Stories, and Quotes

Puerto Rican chef José Andrés has said, "Food is a bridge to the heart of any culture, and in Puerto Rico, that heart beats with the vibrant flavors and welcoming spirit of its cuisine." Green Plantain Pies beautifully illustrate this, bringing the essence of Puerto Rican cuisine to your plate.

Chef Evaluation

These Pastelillos de Plátano Verde embody the rich and diverse flavors of Puerto Rican cuisine. Crispy, golden plantains encase a savory beef filling, creating a delicious and satisfying dish that's perfect for sharing or savoring on your own.

Serving Suggestions

Savor these green plantain pies alongside other Puerto Rican favorites, such as rice and beans (arroz con habichuelas) or a refreshing salad, for a well-rounded meal.

Best Time to Eat

Enjoy Pastelillos de Plátano Verde as a savory snack or a hearty lunch or dinner. Their bold flavors and crispy texture make them an ideal addition to any meal.

Conclusion

Experience the diverse and flavorful cuisine of Puerto Rico with these Fried Green Plantain Pies.

Guatemalan Stuffed Plantain Leaves
(Tamales de Plátano)

Introduction
Journey to Guatemala with this Stuffed Plantain Leaves recipe, known as Tamales de Plátano. This traditional dish combines tender plantain leaves with a savory corn-based filling, creating a delightful fusion of flavors and textures that showcases the essence of Guatemalan cuisine.

Brief History
Tamales have a rich history in Guatemalan culinary culture, dating back to pre-Columbian times when the indigenous Maya people prepared them as offerings to the gods. Over time, tamales evolved to incorporate various ingredients and fillings, with Stuffed Plantain Leaves becoming a beloved staple of Guatemalan gastronomy.

Ingredients
12 large plantain leaves
2 cups masa harina (corn flour)
2 cups chicken broth or vegetable broth
1/2 cup vegetable shortening, melted
1 tsp baking powder
1 tsp kosher salt
1/2 tsp ground black pepper
4 cups cooked and shredded chicken or pork
1 cup tomato sauce
1/2 cup pitted green olives, sliced
1/4 cup raisins
1/4 cup capers

Preparation Steps

Soak the plantain leaves in hot water for 5-10 minutes, or until softened and pliable.

In a large bowl, mix the masa harina, chicken broth, melted vegetable shortening, baking powder, salt, and pepper until well combined. The mixture should be smooth and have a soft dough-like consistency.

Add the shredded chicken, tomato sauce, olives, raisins, and capers to the masa mixture and stir to combine.

To assemble, lay a softened plantain leaf on a clean work surface with the veins facing up. Place about 1/2 cup of the filling mixture in the center of the leaf.

Fold the sides of the leaf over the filling, then fold the ends to create a rectangular packet. Secure the stuffed plantain leaves with kitchen twine or toothpicks.

Fill a large pot with 1-2 inches of water and place a steamer basket or metal rack inside.

Arrange the tamales on the steamer basket or rack, cover with a lid, and steam for 60-75 minutes or until the masa is fully cooked and firm to the touch.

Serve your Guatemalan Stuffed Plantain Leaves with a side of Guatemalan salsa or fresh avocado for a truly authentic experience.

Health Benefits

Plantain leaves are a good source of vitamins, minerals, and antioxidants. When consumed in moderation, these Stuffed Plantain

Leaves can be part of a balanced diet and an enjoyable way to explore Guatemalan cuisine.

Storage and Reheating Information

Keep any remaining tamales in an airtight container and store them in the refrigerator for a maximum of 3 days.
To reheat, steam for 15-20 minutes or until warmed through.

Anecdotes, Stories, and Quotes

Guatemalan chef and culinary ambassador Amalia Moreno-Damgaard has said, "Food is not just about sustenance; it's about celebrating our culture and sharing our stories." Stuffed Plantain Leaves beautifully encapsulate this sentiment, bringing the flavors and traditions of Guatemala to your table.

Chef Evaluation

These Tamales de Plátano embody the rich and diverse flavors of Guatemalan cuisine. Tender plantain leaves envelop a savory filling, creating a delightful and satisfying dish that's perfect for sharing with friends and family.

Serving Suggestions

Enjoy these Stuffed Plantain Leaves alongside other Guatemalan favorites, such as rice, beans, and fresh tortillas, for a well-rounded meal.

Best Time to Eat

Tamales de Plátano can be enjoyed for breakfast, lunch, or dinner. Their versatile flavors and filling nature make them an ideal addition to any meal.

Conclusion

Experience the rich culinary heritage of Guatemala with these Stuffed Plantain Leaves. Each delicious bite is a celebration of the country's vibrant culture and mouth watering flavors.

Colombian Plantain Tostones (Patacones)

Introduction
Immerse yourself in Colombian flavors with this classic Plantain Tostones recipe, known as Patacones. Twice-fried plantain slices are transformed into crispy, golden delights that are both satisfying and versatile. Serve as a snack or a side dish to create a true Colombian culinary experience.

Brief History
Tostones have deep roots in Latin American cuisine, with the origins of this beloved dish tracing back to various regions, including Colombia. Over time, the dish has evolved and become an iconic part of Colombian gastronomy, often served alongside flavorful salsas or guacamole.

Ingredients
4 unripe green plantains
Kosher salt, to taste
Vegetable oil, for frying
Optional garnishes: lime wedges, salsa, guacamole, or hogao (Colombian tomato and onion sauce)

Preparation Steps
Slice the ends off the plantains and cut a shallow slit down the side to help remove the peel. Slide your thumb under the slit to peel off the skin.

Cut the peeled plantains into thick, 1-inch slices.

Fill a deep, heavy-bottomed pot or deep fryer with vegetable oil and heat it to 350°F (175°C).

Carefully place the plantain slices in the hot oil and fry for 2-3 minutes on each side or until they turn a light golden color.

Remove the plantain slices from the oil and drain on a paper towel-lined plate. Allow them to cool slightly before the next step.

Using a tostonera (plantain press) or a flat object like a cutting board, gently flatten each plantain slice to about half its original thickness.

Return the flattened plantain slices to the hot oil and fry for an additional 2-3 minutes or until golden brown and crispy.

Transfer the cooked tostones to a wire rack or paper towel-lined plate to drain any excess oil.

Sprinkle with kosher salt while still hot and garnish with lime wedges, salsa, guacamole, or hogao for a truly authentic Colombian experience.

Health Benefits

Plantains are rich in fiber, potassium, and essential vitamins. When consumed in moderation, these Plantain Tostones can be part of a balanced diet and a delicious way to experience Colombian cuisine.

Storage and Reheating Information

Plantain Tostones are best enjoyed fresh and hot. If needed, store leftovers in an airtight container in the refrigerator and reheat in a preheated 375°F (190°C) oven until warmed through and crispy.

Anecdotes, Stories, and Quotes

As Colombian chef and restaurateur Jamie Rodríguez has said, "Colombian cuisine is a celebration of flavors and traditions, each dish telling a story of our rich cultural heritage." Plantain Tostones are a prime example, showcasing the unique and vibrant flavors of Colombia.

Chef Evaluation

These Patacones perfectly encapsulate the essence of Colombian cuisine. Crispy, golden plantain slices offer a delightful and versatile snack or side dish that complements a variety of flavors and textures.

Serving Suggestions

Pair these Plantain Tostones with traditional Colombian dishes such as Bandeja Paisa or Ajiaco for a complete and authentic culinary experience.

Best Time to Eat

Patacones can be enjoyed at any time of day, whether as a flavorful appetizer, a satisfying side dish, or a delightful snack.

Conclusion

Journey through Colombia's vibrant culinary landscape with these Plantain Tostones. Each crispy, golden bite is a testament to the rich traditions and flavors that make Colombian cuisine so enticing.

Italian Plantain Pizza (Pizza di Platano)

Introduction
Experience a unique fusion of Italian and tropical flavors with this innovative Plantain Pizza recipe. By using plantains as the pizza crust, this dish offers a gluten-free alternative that's both delicious and satisfying.

Brief History
While pizza has its roots in Italy, this Plantain Pizza combines the essence of traditional Italian flavors with the versatile plantain, a staple in Latin American and African cuisines. This inventive twist on classic pizza allows for a delightful culinary fusion.

Ingredients
For the plantain crust:

2 large green plantains

1/2 cup grated Parmesan cheese

1/4 cup almond flour

1/4 tsp kosher salt

1/4 tsp dried oregano

1/4 tsp garlic powder

1 egg, beaten

For the toppings:

1/2 cup pizza sauce

1 cup shredded mozzarella cheese

Additional toppings of choice (pepperoni, vegetables, olives, etc.)

Fresh basil leaves

Preparation Steps

Preheat the oven to 400°F (200°C) and cover a baking sheet with parchment paper.

Peel the green plantains and cut them into large chunks. Place the plantain chunks into a food processor and pulse until they reach a rice-like consistency.

In a large bowl, mix the plantain rice with grated Parmesan cheese, almond flour, salt, oregano, and garlic powder until thoroughly combined.

Add the beaten egg to the mixture and mix until a dough-like consistency is achieved.

Place the dough on the parchment-lined baking sheet and flatten it into a thin, circular crust using your hands or a rolling pin.

Bake the plantain crust for 15-20 minutes or until it begins to turn golden brown.

Remove the crust from the oven and top it with pizza sauce, shredded mozzarella cheese, and any additional toppings of your choice.

Return the pizza to the oven for another 10-15 minutes or until the cheese is melted and bubbling.

Garnish with fresh basil leaves and serve hot, slicing the pizza into wedges for easy enjoyment.

Health Benefits
Plantains offer fiber, potassium, and essential vitamins. This Plantain Pizza provides a gluten-free and nutrient-rich alternative to traditional pizza crust, making it a delicious option for those with dietary restrictions or preferences.

Storage and Reheating Information
Store leftover Plantain Pizza in an airtight container in the refrigerator for up to 3 days. Reheat in a preheated 375°F (190°C) oven until warmed through and crispy.

Anecdotes, Stories, and Quotes
Italian chef and food writer Marcella Hazan once said, "The kitchen is a country in which there are always discoveries to be made." This Plantain Pizza is a prime example, showcasing how combining different culinary traditions can result in delightful new dishes.

Chef Evaluation
Pizza di Platano presents an inventive twist on traditional Italian pizza. The unique plantain crust offers a nutritious and flavorful base for an array of toppings, creating a delicious and satisfying meal.

Serving Suggestions
Serve this Plantain Pizza alongside a fresh Italian salad or antipasto platter for a delightful and well-rounded meal.

Best Time to Eat
This versatile pizza is perfect for a family dinner, a weekend lunch, or a fun appetizer to share at a gathering.

Conclusion

Pizza di Platano is an innovative fusion of Italian and tropical flavors. With its unique plantain crust and customizable toppings, this dish invites you to explore new culinary horizons.

Ghanaian Plantain Porridge (Mutufu Ekado)

Introduction
Embark on a flavorful journey to Ghana with this comforting Plantain Porridge recipe, known as Mutufu Ekado. Combining ripe plantains with spices and vegetables, this dish offers a warm and satisfying taste of West African cuisine.

Brief History
Mutufu Ekado is a beloved staple in Ghana, tracing its roots back to the country's diverse culinary traditions. This dish has evolved over time, with plantains serving as a versatile and nutritious base for a variety of flavors and ingredients.

Ingredients
4 ripe plantains
1/2 cup palm oil
1 medium onion, chopped
1 bell pepper, chopped
1/4 tsp ground ginger
1/4 tsp ground coriander
1/4 tsp ground anise
1/4 tsp red chili flakes (optional)
1 cup water
Kosher salt, to taste
Optional garnishes: chopped cilantro, sliced avocado, and lime wedges

Preparation Steps

Peel the ripe plantains and cut them into 1-inch slices.

In a medium-sized pot, heat the palm oil over medium heat. Add the chopped onion and bell pepper, cooking until softened (about 5-7 minutes).

Stir in the ground ginger, coriander, anise, and red chili flakes (if using). Continue cooking for an extra 2-3 minutes until you can smell the aroma.

Add the sliced plantains and 1 cup of water to the pot, stirring gently to combine all ingredients.

Bring the mixture to a gentle simmer, cover with a lid, and let it cook for 15-20 minutes or until the plantains are tender and easily mashed. Using a potato masher or wooden spoon, mash the cooked plantains until the desired consistency is reached. Add additional water if needed for a thinner porridge.

Season with kosher salt to taste and serve the Plantain Porridge hot, garnishing with chopped cilantro, sliced avocado, and lime wedges for added flavor.

Health Benefits

Plantains are a good source of fiber, potassium, and essential vitamins. This Ghanaian Plantain Porridge offers a nutritious and comforting meal that can be enjoyed by all.

Storage and Reheating Information

Store leftover Mutufu Ekado in an airtight container in the refrigerator for up to 3 days. To reheat on the stovetop, warm over medium heat, stirring occasionally until thoroughly heated. Add water if necessary to achieve the desired consistency.

Anecdotes, Stories, and Quotes

As Ghanaian chef and culinary ambassador Selassie Atadika has said, "Food is a powerful connector to our roots and identity." Plantain Porridge perfectly embodies this sentiment, celebrating the rich and diverse flavors of Ghanaian cuisine.

Chef Evaluation

This Mutufu Ekado showcases the warmth and depth of Ghanaian culinary traditions. The comforting porridge offers a blend of sweet plantains and aromatic spices, creating a satisfying dish that's perfect for sharing with friends and family.

Serving Suggestions

Enjoy this Plantain Porridge alongside a refreshing salad or traditional Ghanaian dishes such as Jollof Rice or Peanut Soup.

Best Time to Eat

Mutufu Ekado is a versatile dish that can be enjoyed for breakfast, lunch, or dinner, providing a comforting and delicious meal at any time of day.

Conclusion

Journey through the vibrant culinary landscape of Ghana with this Plantain Porridge. With its blend of sweet plantains and savory spices, this dish invites you to explore the rich and diverse flavors of West African cuisine.

French Plantain Gratin (Gratin de Plantain)

Introduction
Indulge in the rich, comforting flavors of this French Plantain Gratin, a unique twist on the classic French dish. Combining layers of thinly sliced plantains, cream, cheese, and aromatic herbs, this dish offers an exquisite blend of French and tropical flavors.

Brief History
Gratin has been a staple in French cuisine for centuries, with many regional variations showcasing local ingredients and flavors. This Plantain Gratin offers a fresh take on tradition, incorporating plantains for a delicious fusion of French and global cuisines.

Ingredients
4 medium ripe plantains
2 cups heavy cream
1/2 cup grated Gruyère cheese
1/4 cup fresh chives, chopped
1/4 cup fresh parsley, chopped
1 garlic clove, minced
1/4 tsp freshly grated nutmeg
kosher salt and freshly ground black pepper according to your taste preferences

Preparation Steps
Preheat the oven to 375°F (190°C). Coat a 9x13-inch baking dish with butter or cooking spray.

Peel the plantains and slice them thinly (about 1/8-inch thick).

In a large mixing bowl, whisk together the heavy cream, Gruyère cheese, chives, parsley, minced garlic, and nutmeg. Season with kosher salt and freshly ground black pepper according to your taste preferences.

Layer half of the sliced plantains in the prepared baking dish, slightly overlapping them to create a uniform layer.

Pour half of the cream mixture evenly over the plantain layer.

Add the remaining plantain slices on top, creating another uniform layer, and pour the remaining cream mixture over the top.

Bake the Plantain Gratin for 45-55 minutes or until the plantains are fork-tender and the top is golden and bubbly.

Allow the gratin to cool for 10-15 minutes before serving.

Health Benefits
Plantains offer fiber, potassium, and essential vitamins. When consumed in moderation, this French Plantain Gratin can be enjoyed as part of a balanced diet and a delightful way to experience French cuisine.

Storage and Reheating Information
Store leftover Gratin de Plantain in an airtight container in the refrigerator for up to 3 days. Reheat in a preheated 375°F (190°C) oven until warmed through and crispy on top.

Anecdotes, Stories, and Quotes
French chef and culinary icon Julia Child once said, "The art of French cooking is that it's not just about the ingredients, but how they are combined and cooked." This Plantain Gratin is a testament to this

philosophy, showcasing the harmonious blend of French technique and global flavors.

Chef Evaluation

Gratin de Plantain presents a sophisticated and innovative twist on classic French cuisine. The layers of tender plantains, cream, and cheese create a delightful fusion of sweet and savory flavors, making this dish a standout on any table.

Serving Suggestions

Serve this French Plantain Gratin alongside roasted meats, like chicken or beef, and a fresh green salad for a well-rounded meal.

Best Time to Eat

Gratin de Plantain is a perfect dish for a cozy dinner or a festive celebration, where its comforting and indulgent flavors can be enjoyed by all.

Conclusion

Embark on a culinary adventure with this Plantain Gratin, fusing the rich traditions of French cuisine with the delightful flavors of plantains. With each bite, experience the harmony of ingredients and technique that make this dish a true testament to the art of French cooking.

Italian Plantain Gnocchi (Gnocchi di Platano)

Introduction
Experience a delightful twist on traditional Italian gnocchi with this Plantain Gnocchi recipe. By using plantains instead of potatoes, this dish offers a unique and flavorful take on the classic, making it a perfect option for those seeking a gluten-free alternative.

Brief History
Gnocchi has been a staple in Italian cuisine since ancient Roman times, with various regions of Italy offering their unique take on this versatile dish. This Plantain Gnocchi combines the essence of Italian tradition with the distinctive flavor of plantains, creating a delightful fusion.

Ingredients
2 large ripe plantains
1/2 cup almond flour
1/4 cup tapioca flour
1/2 tsp kosher salt
1 large egg

Preparation Steps
Preheat the oven to 400°F (200°C). Cover a baking sheet with parchment paper.

Peel the ripe plantains and place them on the parchment-lined baking sheet. Bake for 20-25 minutes or until they are tender and slightly caramelized.

Remove the plantains from the oven and let them cool for 5-10 minutes. Mash the plantains until smooth using a potato ricer, food mill, or fork.

Combine the mashed plantains, almond flour, tapioca flour, and kosher salt in a large mixing bowl. Mix until thoroughly combined.

Add the large egg to the mixture, gently incorporating it until a soft dough forms.

Divide the dough into four equal parts. On a lightly floured surface, roll each portion into a long rope about 1-inch in diameter.

Slice the rope into 1-inch pieces using a sharp knife. Roll each piece over the tines of a fork to create the classic gnocchi texture and shape.

In a large pot, bring salted water to a gentle boil. Carefully drop the plantain gnocchi into the water, cooking until they float to the surface (about 2-3 minutes).

Remove the cooked gnocchi with a slotted spoon and serve with your favorite sauce, such as a classic marinara or pesto sauce.

Health Benefits
Plantains offer fiber, potassium, and essential vitamins. This Plantain Gnocchi provides a gluten-free and nutrient-rich alternative to traditional gnocchi, making it an enjoyable option for those with dietary restrictions or preferences.

Storage and Reheating Information
Store uncooked Plantain Gnocchi in an airtight container in the refrigerator for up to 2 days. To freeze, arrange gnocchi on a floured baking sheet and freeze until solid. Place the gnocchi into an airtight

container and freeze for a maximum of 2 months. Cook the frozen gnocchi directly from the freezer.

Anecdotes, Stories, and Quotes

Italian chef Massimo Bottura once said, "Cooking is a language through which we can express our emotions and share our culture." This Plantain Gnocchi is a testament to this idea, combining traditional Italian cuisine with the flavors of plantains for a truly unique culinary experience.

Chef Evaluation

Gnocchi di Platano showcases the adaptability of Italian cuisine, offering a delicious gluten-free alternative to traditional gnocchi. The distinct flavor of plantains adds depth and character to this dish, creating an exceptional culinary fusion.

Serving Suggestions

Serve this Italian Plantain Gnocchi alongside a fresh Italian salad or grilled seasonal vegetables for a delightful and well-rounded meal.

Best Time to Eat

This versatile gnocchi can be enjoyed for lunch or dinner, providing a delicious and satisfying meal any time of day.

Conclusion

Gnocchi di Platano invites you to explore the innovative world of Italian cuisine. Experience the delightful fusion of traditional technique and unique flavors with each bite, as this dish brings a fresh and exciting twist to classic gnocchi.

Mexican Plantain Sopes

Introduction

Embrace the vibrant spirit of Mexico with these Plantain Sopes, a unique twist on the classic Mexican dish. By incorporating ripe plantains into the masa dough, this recipe offers a delightful fusion of flavors that's sure to impress your taste buds.

Brief History

Sopes have been a staple in Mexican cuisine for centuries, with their origins rooted in the country's indigenous cultures. This inventive Plantain Sopes recipe celebrates tradition while introducing new flavors and ingredients.

Ingredients

For the Plantain Masa:

2 cups masa harina

1 ripe plantain, mashed

1/2 tsp kosher salt

1 1/4 cup warm water

For the Sopes Toppings:

Add 2 cups of cooked and shredded chicken or pork to the mixture

Include 1/2 cup of crumbled queso fresco or feta cheese

1/2 cup pickled red onions

1/2 cup chopped fresh cilantro

1/2 cup crema or sour cream

Optional: sliced avocado, lime wedges, and hot sauce

Preparation Steps

In a large mixing bowl, combine masa harina, mashed ripe plantain, and kosher salt. Slowly pour warm water into the mixture and blend until a soft dough forms.

Divide the dough into 8 equal portions, rolling each into a ball.

Place a ball of dough between two sheets of plastic wrap and flatten it into a 1/4-inch thick disk using a tortilla press or rolling pin.

Remove the plastic wrap and gently pinch the edges of the dough to create a rim around the sope.

Heat a lightly oiled skillet or comal over medium heat. Cook the sopes on each side until golden and slightly crispy (about 2-3 minutes per side).

Add shredded chicken or pork, crumbled cheese, pickled red onions, and chopped cilantro on top of each sope.

Drizzle crema or sour cream on top, and garnish with sliced avocado, lime wedges, and hot sauce if desired.

Health Benefits
Plantains are rich in fiber, potassium, and essential vitamins. By incorporating plantains into the masa dough, this Mexican Plantain Sopes recipe offers a nutritious twist on the traditional dish.

Storage and Reheating Information
Store cooked Plantain Sopes in an airtight container in the refrigerator for up to 3 days. Reheat on a skillet or in the oven until warmed through, then add fresh toppings before serving.

Anecdotes, Stories, and Quotes
As Mexican chef and author Diana Sánchez has said, "Mexican food is a reflection of its people: vibrant, colorful, and full of life." This Plantain Sopes recipe perfectly embodies this sentiment, showcasing the rich and dynamic flavors of Mexican cuisine.

Chef Evaluation

Mexican Plantain Sopes offer a delightful and inventive twist on traditional sopes. The fusion of plantains with classic ingredients creates a dish that's both delicious and unique, showcasing the adaptability and creativity of Mexican culinary traditions.

Serving Suggestions

Serve these Plantain Sopes alongside fresh salsa, a crisp green salad, or a refreshing agua fresca for a well-rounded and delightful meal.

Best Time to Eat

Plantain Sopes make an excellent lunch or dinner option, providing a vibrant and satisfying meal to be enjoyed at any time of day.

Conclusion

Explore the rich and diverse flavors of Mexico with this Plantain Sopes recipe. Experience a delightful fusion of tradition and innovation, as each bite invites you to celebrate the vibrant spirit and culinary heritage of Mexico.

Turkish Plantain Kofte

Introduction
Discover the delightful flavors of Turkey with this Plantain Kofte recipe, a unique twist on traditional Turkish meatballs. By incorporating ripe plantains into the mixture, this dish offers a delicious vegetarian alternative that celebrates Turkish culinary heritage.

Brief History
Kofte has been an integral part of Turkish cuisine for centuries, with various regional adaptations highlighting local ingredients and techniques. This Plantain Kofte recipe embraces tradition while introducing new flavors and ingredients to create a one-of-a-kind dish.

Ingredients
2 medium ripe plantains
1/2 cup fine bulgur
1 small onion, grated
1/4 cup fresh parsley, chopped
1/4 cup fresh mint, chopped
2 garlic cloves, minced
1 tsp ground cumin
1 tsp ground coriander
1/2 tsp Aleppo pepper flakes
kosher salt and freshly ground black pepper according to your taste preferences
Olive oil for cooking

Preparation Steps
Preheat the oven to 400°F (200°C). Cover a baking sheet with parchment paper.

Peel the ripe plantains and place them on the parchment-lined baking sheet. Bake for 20-25 minutes or until they are tender and slightly caramelized.

In a large mixing bowl, mash the cooked plantains using a fork or potato ricer.

Add fine bulgur, grated onion, chopped parsley, mint, minced garlic, ground cumin, coriander, Aleppo pepper flakes, kosher salt, and freshly ground black pepper to the bowl. Mix well until thoroughly combined.

Form the mixture into small oval-shaped kofte, about 1 1/2 inches long.

Heat a small amount of olive oil in a skillet over medium heat. Sear the kofte on all sides until golden brown and crispy.

Serve hot with a refreshing yogurt dip or a traditional Turkish salad.

Health Benefits
Plantains are rich in fiber, potassium, and essential vitamins. This Turkish Plantain Kofte recipe offers a delicious vegetarian option packed with nutrients and bold flavors.

Storage and Reheating Information
Store cooked Plantain Kofte in an airtight container in the refrigerator for up to 3 days. Reheat in the oven or on a skillet until warmed through and crispy on the outside.

Anecdotes, Stories, and Quotes
As Turkish chef and food writer Musa Dağdeviren has said, "Turkish cuisine is a rich tapestry of flavors, woven together by history and

tradition." This Plantain Kofte recipe perfectly embodies this sentiment, showcasing the diverse influences and inventive spirit of Turkish culinary heritage.

Chef Evaluation

Plantain Kofte offers a delightful vegetarian twist on traditional Turkish meatballs. The fusion of plantains with classic spices and herbs creates a dish that's both delicious and unique, reflecting the adaptability and creativity of Turkish cuisine.

Serving Suggestions

Serve these Plantain Kofte with a refreshing yogurt dip, traditional Turkish salads, or wrapped in warm pita bread for a delectable and satisfying meal.

Best Time to Eat

Plantain Kofte can be enjoyed for lunch or dinner, providing a flavorful and satisfying dish to be savored at any time of day.

Conclusion

Embark on a culinary journey to Turkey with this Plantain Kofte recipe. Experience a delightful fusion of tradition and innovation, as each bite invites you to explore the rich tapestry of flavors that define Turkish cuisine.

Indian Plantain Kachori

Introduction

Immerse yourself in the vibrant flavors of India with this Plantain Kachori recipe, a unique twist on the classic savory snack. By incorporating ripe plantains into the filling, this dish offers a delightful fusion of flavors and textures, perfect for any occasion.

Brief History

Kachori has been a beloved street food in India for centuries, with various regions putting their unique spin on this crispy and flavorful snack. This Plantain Kachori recipe honors tradition while introducing new ingredients and techniques.

Ingredients

For the Dough:

2 cups all-purpose flour

1/2 cup water

1 tsp kosher salt

2 tbsp vegetable oil

For the Plantain Filling:

2 medium ripe plantains, mashed

1/2 cup yellow moong dal (split mung beans), cooked

1 tsp cumin seeds

1/2 tsp ground turmeric

1/2 tsp garam masala

1/2 tsp red chili powder

kosher salt and freshly ground black pepper according to your taste preferences

Vegetable oil for frying

Preparation Steps

In a large mixing bowl, combine all-purpose flour, water, kosher salt, and vegetable oil to create the dough. Knead until smooth and elastic. Cover the mixture with a damp cloth and let it sit.

In a separate mixing bowl, combine mashed ripe plantains, cooked yellow moong dal, cumin seeds, turmeric, garam masala, red chili powder, kosher salt, and freshly ground black pepper. Mix well until thoroughly combined.

Divide the dough into small, golf-ball-sized portions. Roll each dough portion into a circle about 3-4 inches in diameter.

Place a spoonful of the plantain filling in the center of each dough circle. Bring the edges together to seal the filling inside, creating a small ball shape.

Heat a few inches of vegetable oil in a heavy-bottomed pan over medium heat. Carefully drop the kachoris into the hot oil, frying until golden brown and crispy (about 2-3 minutes per side).

Remove kachoris from the oil and place them on a paper towel-lined plate to drain any excess oil.

Enjoy the dish hot with your preferred chutney or raita.

Health Benefits

Plantains are rich in fiber, potassium, and essential vitamins, while moong dal provides protein and additional nutrients. This Indian Plantain Kachori recipe offers a flavorful and nutritious snack option.

Storage and Reheating Information

Store cooked Plantain Kachori in an airtight container in the refrigerator for up to 3 days. Reheat in the oven or on a skillet until warmed through and crispy on the outside.

Anecdotes, Stories, and Quotes

As Indian chef and author Madhur Jaffrey has said, "Food, like music and language, is a marker of identity, a symbol of culture." This Plantain Kachori recipe perfectly embodies this sentiment, blending traditional Indian flavors with unique ingredients to create a dish that's both delicious and culturally rich.

Chef Evaluation

Plantain Kachori offers a delightful vegetarian twist on the classic Indian snack. The fusion of plantains with traditional spices and flavors creates a dish that's both unique and flavorful, showcasing the adaptability and creativity of Indian cuisine.

Serving Suggestions

Serve these Plantain Kachoris with a tangy chutney or a refreshing raita for a delightful and well-rounded snack.

Best Time to Eat

Plantain Kachori can be enjoyed as a snack or appetizer, providing a satisfying and flavorful treat to be savored any time of day.

Conclusion

Journey through the vibrant flavors of India with this Plantain Kachori recipe. Experience a delightful fusion of tradition and innovation, as each bite invites you to explore the rich culinary landscape that defines Indian cuisine.

American Plantain Grilled Cheese

Introduction
Embark on a culinary adventure across the United States with this Plantain Grilled Cheese recipe. By incorporating sweet and savory fried plantains into a classic grilled cheese sandwich, this dish offers a unique fusion of flavors that's sure to delight your taste buds.

Brief History
Grilled cheese has been a beloved comfort food in the United States for decades, with its origins dating back to the 1920s. This inventive Plantain Grilled Cheese recipe celebrates tradition while introducing new flavors and ingredients to create a one-of-a-kind sandwich.

Ingredients
For the Fried Plantains:
2 ripe plantains, sliced into 1/4-inch thick rounds
2 tbsp vegetable oil
Pinch of kosher salt
For the Grilled Cheese Sandwich:
4 slices of your favorite bread
2 slices of cheddar cheese
2 tbsp butter, softened

Preparation Steps
Warm vegetable oil in a skillet over medium heat.Add sliced plantains and fry until golden brown and caramelized (about 2-3 minutes per side). Warm vegetable oil in a skillet over medium heat.

Spread butter on one side of each bread slice. On the unbuttered side of two bread slices, place a slice of cheddar cheese.
Add fried plantains on top of the cheese, distributing them evenly.

Place the remaining bread slices on top, with the buttered side facing outwards.

Heat a clean skillet over medium heat. Place the sandwiches in the skillet and grill until the bread is golden and the cheese is melted (about 2-3 minutes per side).

Remove grilled cheese sandwiches from the skillet, slice in half, and serve immediately.

Health Benefits
Plantains are rich in fiber, potassium, and essential vitamins. By incorporating fried plantains into a classic grilled cheese sandwich, this American Plantain Grilled Cheese recipe offers a delicious and nutritious meal option.

Storage and Reheating Information
Store cooled Plantain Grilled Cheese in an airtight container in the refrigerator for up to 2 days. Reheat on a skillet or in the oven until warmed through and crispy on the outside.

Anecdotes, Stories, and Quotes
As American chef and author Julia Child has said, "You don't have to cook fancy or complicated masterpieces - just good food from fresh ingredients." This Plantain Grilled Cheese recipe perfectly embodies this sentiment, showcasing the beauty of simple ingredients and innovative twists on classic dishes.

Chef Evaluation
Plantain Grilled Cheese offers a delightful and inventive twist on the classic American sandwich. The fusion of fried plantains with melted cheese creates a dish that's both delicious and unique, reflecting the creativity and adaptability of American cuisine.

Serving Suggestions

Serve these Plantain Grilled Cheese sandwiches with your favorite soup or a fresh green salad for a comforting and satisfying meal.

Best Time to Eat

Plantain Grilled Cheese can be enjoyed for lunch or dinner, providing a flavorful and comforting dish to be savored any time of day.

Conclusion

Embrace the spirit of American cuisine with this Plantain Grilled Cheese recipe. Experience a delightful fusion of flavors and textures, as each bite invites you to celebrate the rich culinary landscape of the United States.

Made in United States
Troutdale, OR
12/13/2024